UNMISSABLE HIKE

WALKING
CHAMONIX
MONT BLANC

by
Andrew
McCluggage

**KNIFE
EDGE**
Outdoor Guidebooks

About the Author

Andrew McCluggage is an outdoor writer and photographer from Northern Ireland. After 20 years as a corporate lawyer, he decided to do something interesting and started writing walking guidebooks.

His first book was Walking in the Briançonnais, covering a beautiful part of the French Alps. Since then, he has written a variety of guidebooks for hiking and trekking.

Other Knife Edge Outdoor Guidebooks written by Andrew include:

- ► Tour du Mont Blanc
- ► Walker's Haute Route: Chamonix to Zermatt
- ► Tour of the Écrins National Park (GR54)
- ► The Mourne Mountains
- ► Trekking the Dolomites AV1
- ► Walking Brittany

The view of the Mer de Glace from Signal Forbes (Walk 1)

KNIFE
EDGE
Outdoor Guidebooks

Publisher: Knife Edge Outdoor Limited (NI648568)
12 Torrent Business Centre, Donaghmore, County Tyrone, BT70 3BF, UK
www.knifeedgeoutdoor.com

©Andrew McCluggage 2020
All photographs: ©Andrew McCluggage 2020
ISBN: 978-1-912933-04-4

First edition 2020

A catalogue record for this book is available from the British Library.

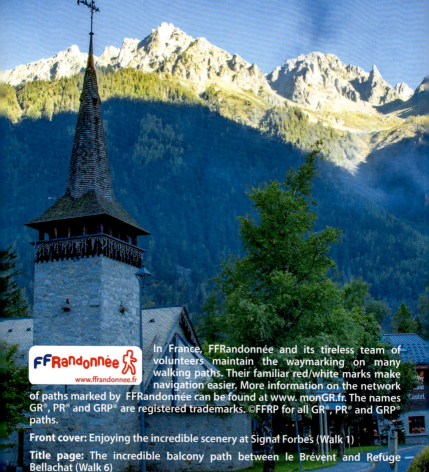

In France, FFRandonnée and its tireless team of volunteers maintain the waymarking on many walking paths. Their familiar red/white marks make navigation easier. More information on the network of paths marked by FFRandonnée can be found at www. monGR.fr. The names GR®, PR® and GRP® are registered trademarks. ©FFRP for all GR®, PR® and GRP® paths.

Front cover: Enjoying the incredible scenery at Signal Forbes (Walk 1)

Title page: The incredible balcony path between le Brévent and Refuge Bellachat (Walk 6)

This page: The village of les Praz de Chamonix

Contents

The fountain in Place
Jacques Balmat, Chamonix

All routes described in this guide have been recently walked by the author and both the author and publisher have made all reasonable efforts to ensure that all information is as accurate as possible. However, while a printed book remains constant for the life of an edition, things in the countryside often change. Trails are subject to forces outside our control: for example, landslides, tree-falls or other matters can result in damage to paths or route changes; waymarks and signposts may fade or be destroyed by wind, snow or the passage of time; or trails may not be maintained by the relevant authorities. If you notice any discrepancies between the contents of this guide and the facts on the ground, then please let us know. Our contact details can be found at the back of this book.

Getting Help

Emergency Services Number: dial 112.

Distress Signal

The signal that you are in distress is 6 blasts on a whistle spaced over a minute, followed by a minute's silence. Then repeat. The acknowledgment that your signal has been received is 3 blasts of a whistle over a minute followed by a minute's silence. At night, flashes of a torch can also be used in the same sequences. **Always carry a torch and whistle.**

Signalling to a Helicopter from the Ground

Help Required
Raise both arms in the shape of a 'Y'

Help Not Required
Raise one arm and extend the other arm down and outwards

WARNING

Hills and mountains can be dangerous places and walking is a potentially dangerous activity. Many of the routes described in this guide cross exposed and potentially hazardous terrain. You walk entirely at your own risk. It is solely your responsibility to ensure that you and all members of your group have adequate experience, fitness and equipment. Neither the author nor the publisher accepts any responsibility or liability whatsoever for death, injury, loss, damage or inconvenience resulting from use of this book, participation in the activity of mountain walking or otherwise.

Some land may be privately owned so we cannot guarantee that there is a legal right of entry to the land. Occasionally, routes change as a result of land disputes.

Descending from le Brévent on Walk 6

Introduction

Autumn colours on Walk 5

Chamonix is the most famous mountain town in the Alps. In fact, it is probably the most famous mountain town in the world and its incredible hiking trails are on the 'bucket list' of most hikers. Its peerless reputation owes everything to the mighty Mont Blanc (MB) which, at 4810m, is the highest peak in Western Europe. Chamonix sits on the floor of the Vallée de l'Arve (Chamonix Valley), just at the foot of MB and is a fabulous base from which to explore the surrounding network of walking paths or plan an ascent of the mountain itself. Walkers, mountaineers and general tourists all stroll through the pedestrian streets of this bustling town, gazing at the beautiful snow-capped summit of MB and its neighbouring peaks and glaciers. After exerting themselves in the mountains, they take the weight off their feet at one of the many bars and restaurants, most of which enjoy fabulous views.

The bars and restaurants are easy to find but it is more difficult to pick out the very finest walks from the sheer volume of hiking options available. This book solves that problem as it is devoted entirely to the Chamonix Valley. Each of the walks here are very different but they all have one thing in common: they provide the hiker with incredible views of the MB Massif and its glaciers. If you undertake a variety of the routes, you can view this sublime range of mountains from every conceivable angle. Both sides of the valley offer amazing walking but they each provide a different perspective. On the W side, you are set back from the MB Massif itself allowing you to enjoy a world-famous panorama of the whole of it. On the E side, however, you can get 'up close and personal' with many of the bright white glaciers that you salivate over from the town itself. Whichever routes you choose, it is fair to say that you will become very well acquainted with the wonderful MB.

Yet although MB is the focal point, continuously drawing the eye, the walking here has much more to offer: snow-frosted summits everywhere you look, incredible high mountain passes (or cols), exquisite alpine pastures, sparkling azure lakes, carpets of wild-flowers, the soothing sound of cow-bells and easy-to-follow paths connecting all of these attractions. This is true 'Sound of Music' scenery. Unforgettable. Unrivalled. Unsurpassable.

With such amazing experiences on offer, it is obvious that you will not be enjoying them alone. The Chamonix Valley is very popular and rightly so. But such popularity is never oppressive. The MB Massif and its surrounds are easily large enough to swallow the many walkers that descend upon them each summer. Get a reasonably early start and you will

The path along the summit ridge of le Prarion (Walk 4)

find yourself largely alone for much of the day. You will pass, or be passed by, other hikers but these meetings can be as fleeting as you wish. And in the bars of Chamonix at the end of the day, you will likely meet some of the people you came across in the mountains.

The walks in this book are designed to cater to all abilities. At first glance, the steepness of the sides of the Chamonix Valley might lead you to believe that all of the walks here would involve brutally steep and sustained climbs. Luckily, however, this is not the case. Chamonix has one of the most comprehensive networks of ski-lifts in the world: the lifts run throughout the summer season, enabling you to gain altitude with little effort.

Consequently, no great level of fitness is required for many of the high trails, which are accessible to all. We will help you use this lift network to best advantage. However, you do not have to use the ski-lifts. Many fitter or more experienced hikers prefer to walk the climbs and we cater for that too: many of the walks have different options depending upon whether or not you wish to use the lifts.

> ### Ask the Author
>
> If you have any questions which are not answered by this book, then you can ask the author on our Facebook Group, 'Walking Chamonix'

Furthermore, down on the valley floor, there is a superb bus and train network which facilitates travel throughout the valley. We have deliberately designed the walks in this book so that they can be used with public transport. In each case, we tell you which bus to take and which train station to get off at, saving you time and effort.

The Chamonix Valley is a big place and there is a lifetime of walks on offer: it is difficult to know where to start and that is where this guidebook comes in. We know that vacation time is precious and that most people do not actually have a lifetime to spend here. We also know that your life is busy and that you have limited time available for research. To make planning easy for you, we have included here only the very finest of the walks available. There are no 'fillers': only the most spectacular routes made the cut. We have 'sifted the wheat from the chaff' so that you do not have to. We will enable you to get the most out of your vacation with the least stress and hassle. The Chamonix Valley is unforgettable and we want your trip to be unforgettable too.

Basic Facts about Mont Blanc

At approximately 4810m, it is the highest peak in Western Europe. The summit is permanently covered in a layer of snow which varies in thickness. Accordingly, it is impossible to determine an exact and permanent summit elevation.

In 1760, Swiss naturalist Horace Bénédict de Saussure, who was obsessed with the Chamonix Valley, offered a reward for the first person to climb MB.

The first recorded ascent was on 8 August 1786 by Jacques Balmat and Michel-Gabriel Paccard. This climb traditionally marks the start of modern mountaineering.

The first woman to reach the summit was Marie Paradis on 14 July 1809.

An estimated 20,000 people now summit MB each year.

The border between Italy and France passes across the summit of MB so it is in fact in both countries. However, the issue of ownership of the summit has been debated since the French Revolution and is apparently still discussed.

The Mont Blanc Tunnel passes through the mountain between Chamonix and Courmayeur (in Italy). It is 11.6km long and opened in 1965.

When to go

Most of the walks in this book take place at high altitude on terrain which is covered by snow for much of the year. Normally, they can be tackled between June and October. Walk 9 is a low-level route which can usually be undertaken at any time of year.

June can be the most beautiful time for walking. The weather is sunny and warm and the peaks are very photogenic, still fully frosted with snow. Summer haze has not yet arrived so visibility is generally excellent with wide-ranging views. And there are carpets of spring wild-flowers. Of course, there is occasionally rain at this time of year but it usually lessens as the season progresses. And there are fewer visitors so the mountains are more peaceful. That said, hiking is becoming more and more popular and the number of early-season walkers seems to increase each year.

However, you should exercise caution as snow can be a problem in June, particularly early in the month: high passes and summits can be covered in snow. Of course this depends on the quantity of snow that fell over the previous winter and the speed of the spring thaw, but in some years high cols and summits can remain snow-covered until early July: this makes some of the walks difficult and/or dangerous. It is impossible to be sure of June conditions in any given year until a few weeks beforehand. However, the risk generally reduces as the month progresses. In snowy conditions, crampons and/or an ice axe might be helpful. There are now some very light, compact crampons available which weigh a mere 300g so carrying them just in case is not the burden it once was. Microspikes are another lightweight option for early-season hikers.

July/August is the main summer season when the high cols are normally passable on foot. It can be hot, sometimes reaching more than 30°C. Mornings often start with clear, sunny skies and heat up as the sun gains height. If there is to be cloud or haze, often this will arrive in the afternoon when thunderstorms are more likely. Start walking early in the morning to complete the main climb while the temperature is cooler. This is the busiest walking season in the Chamonix Valley and it is advisable to make bookings well in advance as accommodation is often full, particularly at weekends. Do not turn up without a reservation and expect to find accommodation.

September is the new June! It can be the best month for walking as the weather is often more settled than in summer. Skies are usually clear and visibility excellent. Daytime temperatures are still warm but evenings get cooler and the days get shorter. The odd flurry of snow is possible, particularly later in the month, but they tend to clear quickly. From the start of September, visitor numbers reduce so the mountains are quieter and there is less demand for accommodation. Some cable cars stop operating in the middle of September.

The Tramway du Mont Blanc (Walk 3)

October is a very beautiful time, with autumn colours on full display in the warm low light. Careful planning is needed to undertake the routes at this time of year. As the month progresses, the possibility of snowfall on the passes and summits increases which could make them impassable or dangerous. Check the weather forecasts carefully. If fresh snow is forecast, do not set out. Furthermore, the days are shorter so it is wise to start walking early: if something were to go wrong, you would have less daylight in which to seek help than in summer. Some cable cars do not operate in October. Generally, October is for more experienced hikers only.

Month	Pros	Cons
June	Pleasant temperatures Frequent sunny skies Good visibility Wild-flower season Fewer visitors	Rainy spells are possible Possibility of snow at altitude Some cable cars do not operate until late June
July/August	Generally fine weather All cable cars and public transport operating	Sometimes hazy Visitor numbers highest
September	Pleasant temperatures Frequent sunny skies Excellent visibility Fewer visitors Autumn colours	Shorter days Cooler evenings Possibility of snow at altitude Some cable cars do not operate after mid-Sept
October	Sometimes crisp clear skies Excellent visibility Fewer visitors	Shortest days It can be cold Possibility of snow at altitude Some cable cars do not operate

Views of MB near les Lacs Noirs (Walk 13)

Where to Base Yourself

There are many small towns and villages in the Chamonix Valley which make excellent bases. Each of them is well-served by public transport enabling easy travel to the start points of the walks in this book. However, often you can hike straight from your doorstep which is a wonderful experience. The key locations where you can stay are listed below but there are plenty of other villages and hamlets in-between.

Chamonix is the principal town in the valley and is a wonderful place to stay. Although it is large and busy, it has a lovely ambiance. The main streets are pedestrianised and packed with cafés, restaurants and outdoor shops: it is a joy to wander along them, admiring the views of MB as you go. There is also an appealing sense of mountaineering history which is felt most strongly as you pass the statues of famous climbers from previous centuries. Here you will rub shoulders with mountaineers, trekkers, trail-runners and plenty of other hikers. It is fair to say that most people want to spend at least a few nights in Chamonix and, to meet this demand, there is plenty of accommodation. Prices are high though.

There is also a very wide variety of activities (other than hiking) on offer: paragliding, rafting, kayaking and mountain-biking to name a few. And Chamonix is served by the pick of the valley's ski-lifts, including the world-famous gondola to Aiguille du Midi which quickly transports you to the incredible altitude of 3842m: it is the highest cable car in Europe so it is an unmissable experience but book online in advance if you wish to avoid the queues (www.montblancnaturalresort.com). Because Chamonix has a central location within the valley, it is the best place to stay if public transport up and down the valley is a priority.

Les Praz de Chamonix is a small village on the northern outskirts of Chamonix. It has hotels, restaurants and a campsite. Because it is at the foot of the recently refurbished Flégère ski-lift, it offers access to some of the finest walking in the valley. It is also well connected by the bus and train networks. The setting is beautiful and there is a lovely riverside path to Chamonix (see Walk 9).

Les Houches is a sprawling town located at the S end of the Chamonix Valley. There is a campsite, hotels, gîtes and apartments for rent. It is served by the Bellevue and Prarion ski-lifts. There is plenty of good walking from the town itself but there is less variety than in Chamonix. Les Houches is on the bus and train networks, however, its location at the southern extremity of the valley means that travel times are longer to the N end of it.

Argentière is a small town which is a quieter alternative to Chamonix and les Houches. The setting beneath the Glacier d'Argentière and the Aiguille Verte is lovely. There is a campsite, a few hotels and gîtes and plenty of apartments for rent. It is served by the Grands Montets cable car so there is some good walking from the town itself. Argentière is on the bus and train networks, however, its location at the northern extremity of the valley means that travel times are longer to the S end of it.

Le Tour is a tiny village at the N end of the Chamonix Valley. The views are lovely and it is served by the Charamillon and Autannes ski-lifts. The walking from the village is excellent. It is on the bus network but its location at the end of the line means that buses are less frequent and travel times to the other parts of the valley are longer. There is only one hotel and one mountain hut to stay at. Furthermore, there are only a few places to eat. If peace and quiet are a priority then le Tour is a good option.

Town/Village	Pros	Cons
Chamonix	The greatest choice of accommodation, restaurants and shops The best access to uplifts and public transport Amazing choice of activities Mountain history Fabulous views Central location within the Chamonix Valley Excellent walking opportunities	Very busy in peak season Less peaceful Expensive
Les Praz de Chamonix	Fabulous views Central location within the Chamonix Valley Walking path to Chamonix centre Excellent walking opportunities	Less peaceful Expensive Fewer places to stay and eat than Chamonix
Les Houches	Plenty of accommodation, restaurants and shops Served by two uplifts Fabulous views Slightly less expensive than Chamonix More peaceful than Chamonix Excellent walking opportunities	Less central location Train station is inconveniently located below the town
Argentière	Plenty of apartments More peaceful than Chamonix and les Houches Fabulous views Less expensive Excellent walking opportunities	Smaller choice of accommodation and restaurants Served by only one uplift Less central location
Le Tour	Very peaceful Fabulous views Excellent walking opportunities	Few places to stay Small choice of places to eat Less central location Public transport less frequent

Using this Book

The walks in this book are only a taste of the many possibilities in this amazing region. You could shorten or lengthen many of the routes to meet your specific needs. Walks have been graded easy, medium, hard or very hard. This is a fairly subjective system (one person's hill is another person's mountain) but you will soon get used to the grading. If there is difficult terrain or significant exposure on a walk, then this can impact its categorisation. The route summary table on pages 33-35 can help you choose a walk.

In this book:

Timings indicate the time required for a reasonably fit walker to complete the route. They do not include any stoppage time. Do not get frustrated if your times do not match those given here: everybody walks at different speeds. You will soon learn how your times compare to ours and you will be able to plan accordingly.

Walking distances are measured in kilometres (km) to match maps and signposts in Continental Europe. However, in the route summary table, we have converted the distances into miles to assist walkers from the US and the UK. One mile equates to 1.6km.

Place names in brackets in the route descriptions indicate the direction to be followed on signposts. For example, "('Chamonix')" would mean that you follow a sign for Chamonix.

Ascent/descent numbers are the aggregate of all the altitude gain or loss (measured in metres) on the uphill or downhill sections of a route. As a rule of thumb, a fit walker climbs 300 to 400m in an hour.

Elevation profiles tell you where the climbs and descents fall on the route. The profile lines have been deliberately drawn in varying thickness purely for aesthetic purposes. Read the elevations off the top of the lines.

Real maps are provided in this guidebook. These are extracts from 1:25,000 scale maps produced by IGN, the French mapping agency. The routes of the walks are marked on the maps.

The following abbreviations are used:

MB	Mont Blanc
TL	Turn left
TR	Turn right
SH	Straight ahead
N, S, E and W, etc.	North, South, East and West, etc.

Exact locations of start points

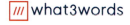

are provided for each walk. To make life easier, we have used the global addressing system devised by what3words. It is one of the simplest ways to talk about location and is much easier to use than traditional coordinate systems. what3words has divided the world into 3mx3m squares, each with a unique 3-word address. You can download the what3words smartphone app (free of charge) from your app store. If you type one of the 3-word addresses into the search box in the app, it will display the location and provide directions to it.

Accommodation

One of Chamonix's many mountaineering statues

Although accommodation is plentiful in the Chamonix Valley, it is wise to book ahead during the busy summer period (July and August), or during public holidays. In addition, the Ultra Trail du Mont Blanc (UTMB), a long-distance trail-running race, takes place each year in the last week of August or first week of September: during the race, accommodation around the Chamonix Valley can be scarce. In June, September and October, there are fewer visitors and you should have no problems finding a beautiful place to stay.

If you stay in paid accommodation within the Chamonix Valley then you will be entitled to a guest card ('Carte d'Hôte') free of charge. Make sure that you ask for the card when you check-in. This card entitles you to free bus and train travel throughout the valley. It also gives you discounts on some car parking charges and many local attractions (such as the Alpine Museum and swimming pool in Chamonix). If you are staying in private accommodation (owned by family or friends) then you can purchase the card for €10 per person per week. Further information is available at www.chamonix.net.

Hotels:
The majority of hotels are in the one to three star categories and quality varies. However, there are also some fabulous four and five star hotels. Normally, hotels offer breakfast and evening meals. 'Half-board' packages (bed, breakfast and dinner) are popular in France and can be good value. Most hotels have their own websites.

Gîtes d'étape:
Traditionally, a gîte would have been comparable to a youth hostel, offering beds in dormitories and evening meals. These days, gîtes are often more upmarket: private rooms are sometimes available and they can be better than some hotels. Most gîtes now have their own websites.

Chambres d'hôte:
Comparable to bed and breakfast accommodation in the UK. Quality can vary widely.

Apartments:
There are many self-catering apartments available to rent in the Chamonix Valley. They can offer great value especially for families or groups. Quality varies from luxurious modern apartments to less expensive older ones. You can book apartments on websites such as www.booking.com and www.airbnb.com.

Refuges:
These are mountain huts which offer dormitory accommodation, meals and alcohol. Refuges are often situated in the heart of the mountains and many are accessible only on foot or by cable car. A night in a refuge can be one of the highlights of a stay in the Chamonix Valley. They are basic but they are good value: a bed, dinner and breakfast should cost around €50-65. If you are lucky, the gardien (manager) may let you sample some homemade Génépy, a potent liqueur made from a plant only found in the high mountains.

Camping

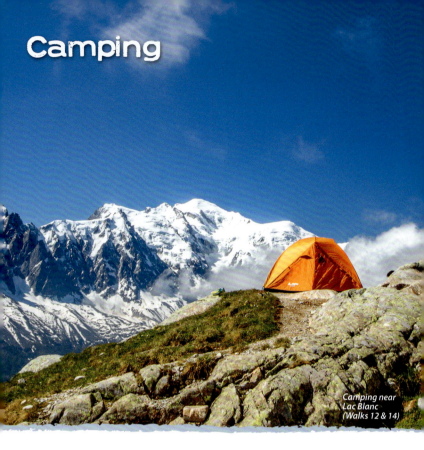

Camping near Lac Blanc (Walks 12 & 14)

The favourable weather means that camping is popular in the Chamonix Valley. There are campsites near Chamonix, les Praz de Chamonix, les Houches and Argentière. They are normally in great locations and are clean and well maintained. Often they do not need to be booked too far in advance. Information for campsites can be found at www.campingfrance.com.

Wild camping is generally prohibited. Local laws provide that it is only permitted to bivouac 'at high altitude' from sunset to sunrise. It is not clear what 'high altitude' means exactly but presumably these rules exist to facilitate climbers and mountaineers who often sleep out on long routes. However, currently overnight bivouac is expressly permitted in the Réserves Naturelles des Aiguilles Rouge which are high up on the W side of the valley (Walks 8, 12, 13 and 14): there are plenty of amazing places to bivouac and many people overnight on the spectacular, exposed ledges near Lac Blanc and Lacs des Chéserys which have grandstand views of the MB Massif. However, do not stray too close to the edge of the cliffs and avoid camping there in bad weather.

All rules and laws are subject to change so check with the local tourist office before setting out. If you get caught breaking the rules, you could get a stiff fine: we warned you! You do hear of walkers who wild camp by being discrete, staying high and only pitching up late in the day. If you do it, make sure that you have checked the rules and do not break them. Always take your rubbish with you (including toilet paper) and bury your toilet waste away from watercourses. Leave no trace.

Food

It could be you! (Walk 1)

The quality of food in France is generally high and the Chamonix Valley is no exception. Walkers are hungry people and most accommodation caters for this providing breakfast, dinner and packed lunches for the following day. Many hotels, gîtes and refuges offer half-board (bed, breakfast and dinner). Evening meals for half-board guests are generally substantial three-course affairs: a starter (often soup) is normally followed by a main course of meat with vegetables, rice, pasta or salad. Half-board will usually finish with dessert or cheese. Vegetarian and vegan options will normally be available on request. Breakfast varies in quality: in hotels it can be a sumptuous affair. However, in refuges which are off the beaten track, it is often the functional minimum of coffee, bread and jam, perhaps with some cheeses or cold meats if you are lucky.

In Chamonix there is a wide variety of restaurants: French restaurants serving local specialities sit alongside burger and pizza joints. Indian and Chinese foods are also available. Smaller towns and villages have a more limited choice.

Local specialities are often rich and filling (and cheese based!): for example, fondues (melted cheese mixed with wine that you dip bread into) and tartiflette (a tasty concoction of potatoes, cream, ham and Reblochon cheese).

For lunch there are sometimes restaurants or mountain huts en route but it is generally more convenient, and cheaper, to picnic amongst the mountains. Fortunately, excellent bread is available in bakeries and supermarkets in the towns/villages: indeed bread is nothing short of a way of life in France. Supermarkets and local shops stock a wide range of fantastic cheeses and cold meats. Alternatively, you can normally buy packed lunches at hotels and gîtes: order them the night before. Be conscious of shop opening hours: outside the main centre of Chamonix, they will often close for a long lunch (somewhere between 12 and 3pm) and then open for a few hours in the late afternoon. If you arrive in a village late then the shops may all be closed.

Getting There

An ibex in front of MB (Walk 14)

By air: the closest international airport to Chamonix is Geneva in Switzerland. See below for on-travel from Geneva airport. Lyon airport is another possibility as you can travel by train from there to the Chamonix Valley (see below).

By train: most towns and villages in the Chamonix Valley are accessible by the Mont Blanc Express linking St Gervais-le Fayet in France with Martigny in Switzerland: from St Gervais, it takes 45min to get to the Chamonix Valley. To get to St Gervais, you can use the recently built Léman Express: a direct line from Geneva taking 1.75hr. You can also travel by train to St Gervais from Paris Gare de Lyon (via Bellegarde or Lyon Part-Dieu): these train services could be linked with the Eurostar from London or a flight to Paris.

By car: you can take a car to France by ferry from a number of different ports in Ireland or the UK. Alternatively, take a car on the train from the UK through the channel tunnel (www.eurotunnel.com). The drive from the French ports to Chamonix should take 8–9hr. From Calais or Dunkirk, the road to Reims can be preferable to avoid the busy Paris ring road. Usually there are spacious car parks at the start points of the walks. However, parking in the town centres of Chamonix, les Houches and Argentière can be a challenge. In Chamonix, you may only leave your car at road sides for 24 hours. Fortunately, however, there are some large car parks just outside Chamonix town centre, although they can be expensive: some car parks offer a discount with a 'Carte d'Hôte' (see Accommodation).

Getting to the Chamonix Valley from Geneva Airport

Minibus Transfers: this is the best way of getting to the Chamonix Valley. A number of companies offer shared and private transfers throughout the day which are scheduled to depart shortly after flights land. They must be booked in advance and take about 90min. They will normally drop you off at your accommodation.

Bus: scheduled buses to Chamonix run a number of times each day. Advance booking is recommended.

Train: you can travel to Chamonix by train from Geneva Airport but it takes 3-4hr and is quite expensive. You have to change two or three times. Take the train from Geneva Airport to Geneva Cornavin. Then change onto the Léman Express (see above) to St Gervais. From St Gervais, change onto the Mont Blanc Express (see 'Getting Around the Chamonix Valley') to travel to the Chamonix Valley.

Further information:

Minibus Transfers: www.mountaindropoffs.com

Trains: www.en.oui.sncf (France); www.sbb.ch (Switzerland)

Buses: www.easybus.com; wwwblablabus.com

The amazing balcony path on Walk 17

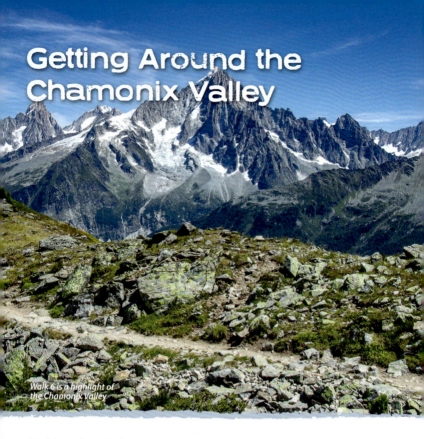

Getting Around the Chamonix Valley

Walk 6 is a highlight of the Chamonix Valley

All of the walks in this book are accessible by public transport: bus, train and/or cable car.

Bus: there is a comprehensive bus system covering most of the Chamonix Valley. The buses are free if you have a Carte d'Hôte (see 'Accommodation'). Details of the lines relevant for the walks in this book are set out on pages 17 and 18. Timetables and routes are subject to change. For further information, see www.chamonix.net.

Train: the Mont Blanc Express runs hourly between St Gervais-le Fayet in France and Martigny in Switzerland. It starts at around 07:00. You can find up-to-date timetables at www.en.oui.sncf.

Useful stops include: les Houches (Walks 3, 4 and 5), les Bossons (Walk 2), Aiguille du Midi (Walk 1), Chamonix (Walks 6, 7, 8, 9, 11 and 13), les Praz (Walks 10, 11, 12, 13 and 20), les Tines (Walk 19) and Argentière (Walk 18). A simplified diagram with the relevant stops is set out below.

Bus Route	Relevant Stops	Dates of Operation	Frequency
Line 1	**Le Prarion** (Walk 4) – **Bellevue** (Walk 3) – **les Houches** – **la Griaz** (Walk 5) – **Chamonix Sud** (Walk 1) – **Chamonix Centre** (Walks 6, 7, 8, 9, 11 and 13) – **les Praz de Chamonix** (Walks 10, 11, 12, 13 and 20)	All year	At least one bus each hour between 06:30 and 20:00. Frequency increases in peak season
Line V1	**Le Prarion** (Walk 4) – **Bellevue** (Walk 3) – **les Houches** – **la Griaz** (Walk 5) – **Chamonix Sud** (Walk 1) – **Chamonix Centre** (Walks 6, 7, 8, 9, 11 and 13) – **Aiguille du Midi** (Walk 1)	End June to start Sept	Four times each day from 09:15
Line 2	**Glacier des Bossons** (Walk 2) – **Chamonix Sud** (Walk 1) – **Chamonix Centre** (Walks 6, 7, 8, 9, 11 and 13) – les **Praz de Chamonix** (Walks 10, 11, 12, 13 and 20) – **le Lavancher** (Walk 19) – l**es Grands Montets** (Walk 18) – **Argentière** – **Montroc** - **le Tour** (Walks 16 and 17)	All year	At least one bus each hour between 06:45 and 20:00. Frequency increases in peak season
Line V2	**Aiguille du Midi** (Walk 1) – **Chamonix Sud** (Walk 1) – **Chamonix Centre** (Walks 6, 7, 8, 9, 11 and 13) – **les Praz de Chamonix** (Walks 10, 11, 12, 13 and 20) – **le Lavancher** (Walk 19) – **Argentière** – **Montroc** - **le Tour** (Walks 16 and 17)	End June to start Sept	Four times each day from 09:25
Line 3	**Bellevue** (Walk 3) – **les Houches** – **la Griaz** (Walk 5) – **Chamonix Sud** (Walk 1) – **Chamonix Centre** (Walks 6, 7, 8, 9, 11 and 13) – **Aiguille du Midi** (Walk 1)	All year	Four times each day from 07:00
Line 21	**Argentière** - **Col des Montets** (Walks 14 and 15)	End June to start Sept	Six times each day from 09:20
Le Mulet	Chamonix town centre shuttle (free of charge)	All year	Every 12 to 20min depending upon the season. From 08:00 to 19:00

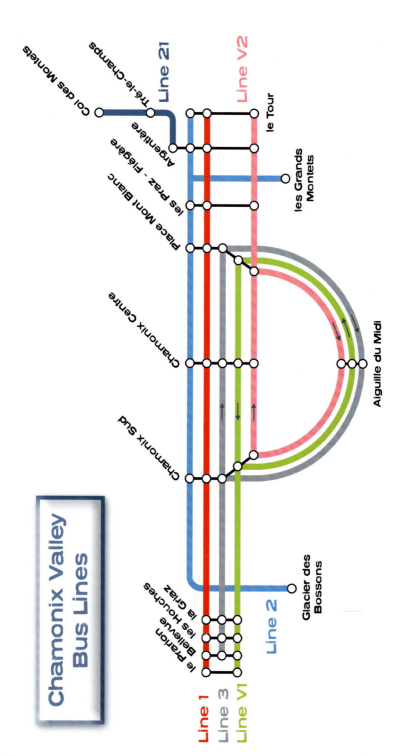

Chamonix Valley
Bus Lines

Line 1
Line 3
Line V1
Line 2

Line 1
Line 21
Line V2

Col des Montets
Tré-le-Champs
Argentière
les Praz - Flégère
Place Mont Blanc
Chamonix Centre
Chamonix Sud
le Tour
les Grands Montets
Aiguille du Midi

le Pranon
Bellevue
les Houches
la Griaz
Glacier des Bossons

18

Superb views of the Aiguilles Rouges on Walk 17

Cable Cars

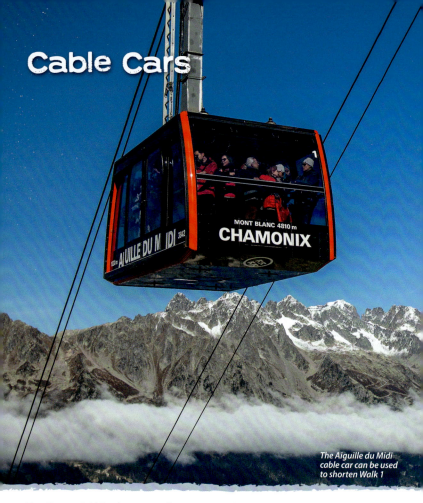

The Aiguille du Midi cable car can be used to shorten Walk 1

The Chamonix Valley has an excellent network of ski-lifts and many of them open during the summer hiking season. You can use them to access many of the walks in this book. Sometimes they help you to avoid a climb and in other cases they save you from a knee-jerking descent. Often they enable the less fit to undertake high altitude walks which would otherwise be accessible only by very fit and experienced hikers.

If you only wish to use one or two lifts during your stay, then purchase tickets individually at the lift stations: there is no discount for advance booking. However, if you wish to use a number of lifts on the same day (or on consecutive days) then the Mont Blanc Multi-Pass can make sense. The pass gives you unlimited use of the Chamonix Valley's lifts (including the expensive Aiguille du Midi) and the more days you buy, the cheaper the daily rate will be. A Multi-Pass is also available for non-consecutive days. You can buy the passes at the lift stations or on the internet. There are some internet discounts available for advance purchases but it can make sense to wait until you are sure the weather will be favourable before purchasing: there are no refunds if the weather is poor!

The available uplifts are listed below: the dates and times of operation are approximate only and change from year to year. Further information, including timetables and Multi-Pass pricing, is available at www.chamonix.net and www.montblancnaturalresort.com.

Location	Cable Car	Relevant Walk Numbers	Approximate Dates of Operation (inclusive)	Approximate times of first ascent and last descent
Les Houches	Bellevue	3	June to mid-Sept	08:00 17:30
Les Houches	Prarion	4	June to mid-Sept	09:00 17:00
Les Bossons	Télésiège du Glacier des Bossons	2	Mid-June to mid-Sept	08:30 18:30
Chamonix	Aiguille du Midi	1	May to Oct	06:30 to 08:00 16:30 to 18:00
Chamonix	Montenvers Tramway	1 and 20	May to Sept Mid-Oct to Nov	08:00 to 10:00 16:30 to 18:30
Chamonix	Planpraz/Brévent	6, 7, 8, 11 and 13	June to mid-Sept	08:10 to 08:30 16:45 to 17:45
Les Praz de Chamonix	La Flégère/Index	11, 12 and 13	June to mid-Sept	08:10 to 08:30 16:45 to 17:45
Argentière	Grands Montets	18	At the date of press, the lift was closed due to fire	At the date of press, the lift was closed due to fire
Le Tour	Charamillon/Autannes	16 and 17	Mid-June to mid-Sept	08:30 to 09:00 16:45 to 17:15

On the Trail

Enjoying Chamonix's pedestrian streets

Weather

The Alps have a relatively dry and predictable climate compared to some other mountainous regions (such as those in the UK). However, conditions can still change quickly so be prepared for rain. Furthermore, snow is always possible on cols and summits, even in the middle of summer. Mountains can be dangerous so treat them with respect and caution, even if the weather forecast is favourable.

The region has a number of micro-climates with the weather often differing from valley to valley. It is possible therefore to find blazing sunshine on one side of a pass and cloud or rain over the other side.

Always get a weather forecast before setting out. Meteo France, the French meteorological office, provides national, regional and local forecasts at www.meteofrance.com. It also has an excellent smartphone app which provides, free of charge, regularly updated local forecasts. Many other internet sites and apps also provide forecasts, with a varying degree of reliability. Local forecasts are also displayed at tourist information offices and refuges.

Maps

The best sheet maps for walking in the Chamonix Valley are the 1:25,000 scale maps produced by IGN, the French mapping agency. In the introduction for each walk, we have indicated which IGN sheet map would be used for the route. Two sheets are required to cover the whole valley: 3531ET St-Gervais-les-Bains and 3630OT Chamonix-Mont-Blanc.

We have used extracts from these sheet maps for the route maps in this book. Although our maps normally enable you to navigate the route, a sheet map can be invaluable, particularly in bad weather. Also, with a sheet map you get a better feel for the geography of the region as it helps you to identify landmarks sighted along the way.

However, perhaps the best overall solution is to combine the real maps provided in this book with IGN's excellent smartphone app: it provides 1:25,000 maps for the whole of France for around £20/$30. The app uses GPS to show your location and direction on the map.

Paths and Waymarking

The routes mostly use clear paths which are easy to follow. Often, there are waymarks (painted on trees and rocks) and signs to assist. Waymarking varies in quality and is at the mercy of the environment: markings can fade or become obscured by rockfalls and landslides. As a rule of thumb, generally keep on a path unless told otherwise.

If you see mountain-biking signs, usually indicated by the letters 'VTT' ('Vélo Tout Terrain'), then take care: mountain-bikes are fast, and often quiet, and a collision between a walker and a mountain-bike could be serious.

Water

Drinking water in the Alps is the subject of regular debate. Except in very dry seasons or towards the end of September, water is usually plentiful in rivers and streams. There are also fountains in most towns and villages and at refuges. Many walkers regularly drink untreated water from these sources without any issues. However, others insist upon filtering or treating the water first to minimise the risk of contaminants. You will have to weigh up the risks and make up your own mind. If, like many, you do decide to drink the water untreated, there are a few rules that you should follow to reduce any risk:

▶ Avoid water where there is evidence nearby of animals, especially cows or sheep: carcasses (of dead animals) or faeces can cause contamination

▶ Do not collect water downstream from buildings or grazing areas

▶ Only drink from moving water. The faster the better

▶ The bigger the river/stream the better

▶ Generally the higher the altitude the better

If you do wish to treat your water, this can be done by way of portable filters, steripens or purification chemicals. The effectiveness of the different products and methods varies and is beyond the scope of this book so do your research before your trip.

Also remember that availability of water at fountains and streams may vary depending upon the season: generally water courses are fullest in June and decline throughout the walking season. It is good practice to fill your water bottles each day before leaving your accommodation. Start with at least 1.5 litres per person.

A typical signpost (Walk 5)

What to Take

The suspension bridge crossed on Walk 3

On any walk, you should be properly equipped for the worst terrain, and the worst weather conditions, which you could encounter: rain, cold and possibly snow. Being cold and wet at high altitude is unpleasant and can be dangerous. However, the dilemma is that you should also consider weight and avoid carrying anything unnecessary. The heavier your pack, the harder the climbs will be. Fortunately, modern equipment helps with this dilemma: there is some fantastic light-weight kit available now. Layering of clothing is the key to warmth. Do not wear cotton: it does not dry quickly and gets cold.

Recommended Basic Kit

Boots/Shoes	Good quality, properly fitting and worn in. Some hike in trail-running shoes but others prefer light boots with ankle support.	
Socks	Good quality, quick drying walking socks. Wash them regularly and change them daily, helping to avoid blisters.	
Waterproof jacket and trousers	Waterproof and breathable. Some people do not bother with waterproof trousers but we like to carry light ones just in case.	
Base layers	T-shirts and underwear of man-made fabrics/merino wool which wick moisture away from your body.	
Fleeces	It can be cold at altitude even in summer. Man-made fabrics.	
Shorts/Trousers	Light walking trousers are normally adequate in summer. In autumn you may need something warmer. Convertible ones are practical as you can remove the legs on warm days.	
Warm hat and gloves	Even in summer it can be cold at altitude, especially in the evening and early morning.	

Down jacket	Even in summer it can be cold at altitude, especially in the evening and early morning.	
Rucksack	Get a light one. A small pack will be adequate to carry your rain jacket and some food. Well-padded shoulder straps and waist band. Much of the weight of the pack should sit on your hips rather than your shoulders.	
Waterproof pack liner	Rucksacks are not very waterproof. A liner will keep your gear dry if it rains.	
Whistle	For emergencies. Many rucksacks have one incorporated into the sternum strap.	
Head-torch with spare batteries	It is good practice to carry a head-torch for emergencies. This can help you if you get caught out late and enables you to signal to rescuers.	
Basic first-aid kit	Including plasters, a bandage and antiseptic wipes.	
Map and compass	For maps see above. A GPS unit or a smartphone app can be a useful addition but they are no substitute for a map and compass: after all, batteries can run out and electronics can fail.	
Knife	Such as a Swiss Army knife. You are going to need to cut that cheese!	
Sunglasses, sun hat, sunscreen and lip salve	The sun in France is strong so do not set out without these items.	
Walking poles	These transfer weight from your legs onto your arms, keeping you fresher. They also save your knees (particularly on descents) and can reduce the likelihood of falling or twisting an ankle.	
Phone and charger (with EU adapter)	A smartphone is a very useful tool on a walking trip. It can be used for emergencies. Furthermore, apps for weather, mapping and hotel booking are invaluable. It can also replace your camera to save weight.	
Space blanket or emergency bag	Very light but it could save your life.	
Food	Carry some emergency food. Energy bars, nuts and dried fruit are all good.	
Water	Start each day with at least 1.5 litres of water per person. Hydration packs with tubes facilitate more effective hydration by enabling drinking on the move. Bring a filter or purification tablets if required.	

Safety

Paragliding above the Glacier du Tour (Walk 17)

On a calm summer's day the Alps are paradise. But a sudden weather shift or an injury can change things dramatically so treat the mountains with respect and be conscious of your experience levels and physical capabilities. The following is a non-exhaustive list of recommendations:

► The fitter you are at the start of your trip, the more you will enjoy the walking

► Before you set out each day, study the route and make plans based upon the abilities of the weakest member of your party

► Get a weather forecast (daily if possible) and reassess your plans in light of it. Avoid exposed routes if the weather is uncertain

► Start early to avoid ascending during the hottest part of the day and to allow more surplus time in case something goes wrong

► Bring a map and compass and know how to use them

► It can be sensible to tell your accommodation where you are going and what time you expect to return. If you do not return then they can raise the alarm

► Carry surplus food and clothing for emergencies

► Never be too proud to turn back if you find the going too tough or if the weather deteriorates

► Do not stray from the route so as to avoid getting lost and to help prevent erosion of the landscape

► Avoid exposed high ground in a thunderstorm. If you get caught out in one then drop your walking poles and stay away from trees, overhanging rocks, metal structures and caves. Generally accepted advice is to squat on your pack and keep as low as possible

► In the event of an accident, move an injured person into a safe place and administer any necessary first-aid. Keep the victim warm. Establish your exact coordinates and, if possible, use your cell-phone to call for help. The emergency numbers are set out on page 1. If you have no signal then send someone for help

► Mountain-biking is popular in the Alps so watch out. A collision with a bike would not be pleasant

Avoiding the crowds

Climbing the ridge to Aiguillette des Houches (Walk 5)

The Chamonix Valley is one of the finest mountain destinations in the world. Accordingly, it is no surprise that it is very busy in summer. The walks in this book feature locations of such exquisite beauty that you will have to share them with others. However, there are things that you can do to help you avoid the bulk of the crowds. Here are our top tips:

▶ **Get out of bed early:** if you start walking at first light then you will be one of the first on the trail. You should get a couple of hours of hiking under your belt before most people start. Furthermore, if you start ahead of the pack then you will stay ahead of it for much of the day. Frustratingly, most accommodation does not serve breakfast until 07:00 which makes it difficult to get on the trail before 08:00: consequently, most people start walking after that time. However, you can use this frustrating fact to your advantage to enjoy the mountains in solitude (for at least part of the day): either forget about having breakfast at your accommodation or ask if they will leave out some basic breakfast foods for you. If you are going to make your own breakfast, then buy food in a supermarket the day before.

▶ **Make sure that you are on the first uplift:** if the walk you wish to do uses a ski-lift to get to the start, then take the first lift of the day. You will be among the first people on that particular trail so you can get ahead of the pack. Arrive at the lift station 10min early to ensure that you get a space in the first car.

▶ **Choose the less popular routes:** places like le Brévent (Walks 6 and 7) and Montenvers (Walks 1 and 20) are magnificent but they are on everybody's bucket list. Consequently, they can get very busy, particularly later in the day. There are, however, many walks which are just as beautiful but are less popular because they do not include 'big name' destinations. For example, le Prarion (Walk 4), les Lacs Noirs (Walk 13), Lac Cornu (Walk 8) and Aiguillette des Posettes (Walk 15) are normally less busy.

▶ **Walk in the early or late season:** in June, September and October there are usually fewer visitors and the trails are quieter. In particular, in late September and October, the weather can be spectacular yet the trails will be practically deserted. The snag is that some of the cable cars may not operate in these periods (see 'Cable Cars').

▶ **Avoid weekends:** locals come out to play at weekends so the trails are busier.

▶ **Make use of the network of mountain huts:** by staying in refuges high up in the mountains, you can start walking the high trails early the following morning before the masses arrive by cable car. Refuge du Lac Blanc and Refuge la Flégère in particular have superb locations high above the valley which are next to plenty of trails (including Walks 11, 12, 13 and 14).

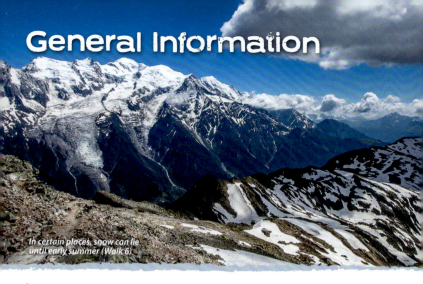

General Information

In certain places, snow can lie until early summer (Walk 6)

Language: French is the first language, however, English is widely spoken in the Chamonix Valley. When in another country, it is good manners to make an effort to say 'hello' in that country's language. If you do so, then you will get a much more positive and friendly response from locals on the trail and off it.

Charging electronic devices: Continental 2-pin plugs are used so visitors from outside Continental Europe will need an adapter.

Money: France uses the Euro(€). There are ATMs in most towns but not in small villages. Credit cards are accepted widely.

Visas: Citizens of the European Union do not need a visa to visit France. At the time of writing, citizens of Australia, New Zealand, Canada and the US do not need a visa for stays of up to three months. Brexit may change things for UK citizens but, at the time of writing, the situation is still unclear.

Cell-phones: There is cell-phone reception almost everywhere in the Chamonix Valley. However, in the mountains, do not rely on it absolutely. 4G services are widely available so access to the internet from smartphones is normally possible.

International dialling codes: The country code for France is +33. If dialling from overseas, the first 0 in the French area code is omitted.

Wifi: Most hotels and gîtes now have wifi. Refuges do not.

Insurance: Mountain rescue services may not be free and therefore it is wise to have adequate insurance which covers hiking. Visitors from the UK should also make sure that they have the free European Health Insurance Card (EHIC) but remember that often this will only cover part of your medical treatment so insurance is still recommended. Also, the EHIC will not cover any rescue itself. After Brexit, it is likely that the EHIC card will become a thing of the past for UK citizens: in such circumstances, private insurance will become even more important.

Emergencies: The emergency telephone number is 112.

Ticks: As is often the case in Europe, ticks may be present. They can carry Lyme disease or tick-borne encephalitis so check yourself regularly. Remove ticks with tweezers (making sure you get all of it out) and then disinfect the area.

Wildlife

A young Ibex seen on Walk 12

Early morning is the best time for seeing wildlife and the first party on the trail has the best chance of a sighting.

Ibex: A member of the goat family with long scimitar-shaped horns. It was saved from extinction by the Savoy kings who banned most hunting in 1821 and created a royal reserve in 1856 (which finally became Italy's Gran Paradiso National Park). After a series of reintroductions in the 20th century, they are now common in the French Alps.

Chamois: Another type of mountain goat which is smaller than the ibex and is widespread in the Alps. It has shorter horns which do not have deep ridges. Chamois are frequently spotted in herds. They are much more wary of humans than ibex.

Deer: Various species are common below the tree-line. Look out for them in forests early in the morning.

Marmots: Everyone loves these fat rodents which are easily spotted in summer when they graze relentlessly to put on layers of fat to last the long winter hibernation. They live in colonies in grassy parts of the mountains, often standing upright on their hind legs like a meerkat. They whistle as you approach to warn their colony of an intruder.

Wild Boar: A member of the pig family with small tusks. They are common in forests but hard to spot. In the unlikely event that you see one, keep your distance because they can be dangerous.

Wolves: Hunted to extinction in France in the 1930s. In recent decades, conservation efforts in Italy increased their numbers and many have now crossed the border into France through the mountains. They are protected but their presence is controversial and particularly unpopular with shepherds who lose many sheep to them. They are more common in the Alps further south, where they are occasionally spotted by walkers.

Other mammals: Squirrels, foxes, badgers and mice are fairly common below the tree-line.

Marmots are plentiful!

Fish: Species of trout are found in rivers, streams and lakes.

Ptarmigan: A grouse-like bird. Its plumage is white in the winter and largely brown in the summer.

Golden Eagle (pictured left): During the hot parts of the day, they can sometimes be seen circling in the thermals to gain altitude as they scan the ground for prey.

Reptiles: There are some snakes including vipers and adders (which are both venomous): if you spot one, keep your distance. There are also lizards, frogs and salamanders.

Ibex have special hooves enabling them to traverse steep rock faces (Walk 14)

Flowers

Doronico or
Leopard's Bane

The Alps are home to thousands of plant species including the incredible wild-flowers. June is a fabulous month for flowers, which wait patiently throughout the winter for the snow to clear and then rapidly spring to life. At this time, carpets of different colours cover the slopes and pastures. Although spring is the peak time for flowers, there are still plenty throughout the summer. Look out for the following:

Alpenrose: A bright pink member of the Rhododendron family which coats the slopes at altitude in June/July.

Edelweiss: Probably the most famous alpine plant, perhaps because it has a song named after it. This rare white flower is striking and hard to spot because it only grows at high altitude (1800–3300m).

Houseleek: A beautiful pink flower which grows on rocks above 1600m. It blooms in August.

Alpine Poppy: This bright yellow flower loves limestone scree and blooms in July/August.

Alpenrose

Edelweiss

Houseleek

Alpine Willowherb

Gentian

Alpine Poppy

Views of Chamonix from Refuge Bellachat (Walks 5 and 6)

Walk No	Walk Name	Grade	Time	Distance (km)	Distance (miles)	Total Ascent (m)	Total Ascent (ft)	Max. Altitude (m)	Max. Altitude (ft)
1	Mer de Glace: the Connoisseur's Route	Very Hard	8	18.2	11.3	1412	4633	2233	7326
	Variant A	Medium	4.75	12.6	7.8	261	856	2310	7579
	Variant B	Hard	6.25	12.9	8.0	1412	4633	2233	7326
	Variant C	Medium	3	7.1	4.4	261	856	2310	7579
2	La Jonction	Very Hard	7.5	17.2	10.7	1618	5309	2589	8495
	Variant A	Hard	6	13.2	8.2	1268	4160	2589	8495
3	Le Nid d'Aigle	Hard	6.5	15.8	9.8	1100	3609	2372	7783
	Variant A	Medium	3.75	10.5	6.5	472	1549	2372	7783
4	Le Prarion	Medium	3.5	8.5	5.3	157	515	1969	6460
5	Aiguillette des Houches	Hard	6.5	13.2	8.2	1040	3412	2285	7497
6	The Mont Blanc Balcony	Medium	3.5	8.8	5.5	15	49	2525	8285

Walk No	Walk Name	Grade	Time	Distance (km)	Distance (miles)	Total Ascent (m)	Total Ascent (ft)	Max. Altitude (m)	Max. Altitude (ft)
7	Col du Brévent	Medium	1.75	3	1.9	555	1821	2525	8285
	Variant A	Hard	5.25	11.80	7.3	570	1870	2525	8285
	Variant B	Very Hard	7	16.60	10.6	788	2585	2525	8285
	Variant C	Hard	3.5	7.80	5.1	773	2536	2525	8285
8	Lac Cornu	Hard	3.5	7	4.4	553	1814	2414	7920
9	Chamonix River Loop	Easy	3	9.9	6.2	105	345	1084	3557
10	Chalet de la Floria	Easy	2.25	5.8	3.6	315	1034	1367	4485
11	Grand Balcon Sud: La Flégère to Planpraz	Medium	1.75	5.2	3.2	293	961	2075	6808
12	Lac Blanc (from La Flégère)	Hard	3.25	6.5	4.0	680	2231	2385	7825
	Variant A	Medium	2.5	6.5	4.0	172	564	2385	7825
13	Les Lacs Noirs	Hard	3.5	7.2	4.5	382	1253	2535	8317
	Variant A	Hard	5.25	12	7.5	478	1568	2535	8317

Walk No	Walk Name	Grade	Time	Distance (km)	Distance (miles)	Total Ascent (m)	Total Ascent (ft)	Max. Altitude (m)	Max. Altitude (ft)
14	Lac Blanc: the Connoisseur's Route	Very Hard	7.75	18	11.2	1415	4643	2352	7717
15	Aiguillette des Posettes	Hard	4.5	10.1	6.3	860	2822	2201	7221
16	Croix de Fer	Very Hard	5	12.9	8.0	970	3183	2343	7687
	Variant A	Hard	3.25	8.6	5.3	238	781	2343	7687
17	Refuge Albert 1st	Medium	4.25	9.2	5.7	566	1857	2702	8865
18	Glacier d'Argentière	Hard	6	13.7	8.5	1110	3642	2338	7671
	Variant A	Medium	3.5	8.2	5.1	389	1276	2338	7671
19	Le Chapeau	Medium	3.5	7.3	4.5	625	2051	1844	6050
20	Mer de Glace (via Buvette des Mottets)	Hard	4.75	11.1	6.9	815	2674	1913	6277
	Variant A	Medium	2.75	5.5	3.4	815	2674	1913	6277

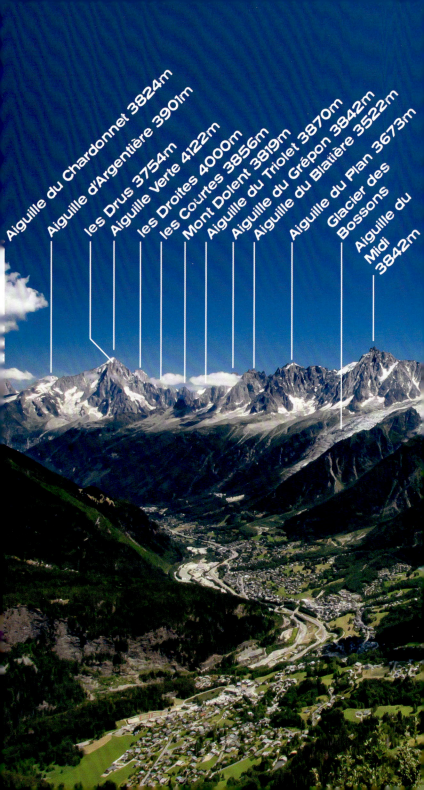

Aiguille du Chardonnet 3824m
Aiguille d'Argentière 3901m
les Drus 3754m
Aiguille Verte 4122m
les Droites 4000m
les Courtes 3856m
Mont Dolent 3819m
Aiguille du Triolet 3870m
Aiguille du Grépon 3842m
Aiguille du Blatière 3522m
Aiguille du Plan 3673m
Glacier des Bossons
Aiguille du Midi 3842m

Route Descriptions

Glacier de Taconnaz

Mont Blanc du Tacul 4248m

Mont Maudit 4465m

Mont Blanc 4812m

Glacier de Bionnassay

Aiguille de Bionnassay 4052m

A panorama of the Chamonix Valley from le Prarion (Walk 4)

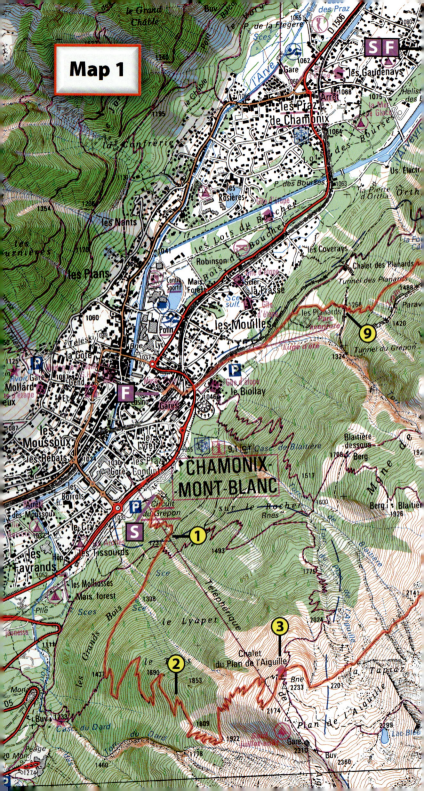

Views of the W side of the Chamonix Valley from the incredible balcony

	Main Route	Variant A	Variant B	Variant C
Time	8:00	4:45	6:15	3:00
Distance	18.2km 11.3 miles	12.6km 7.8 miles	12.9km 8.0 miles	7.1km 4.4 miles
Ascent	1412m 4633ft	261m 856ft	1412m 4633ft	261m 856ft
Descent	1412m 4633ft	1489m 4885ft	535m 1755ft	612m 2008ft
Maximum Altitude	2233m 7326ft	2310m 7579ft	2233m 7326ft	2310m 7579ft
Grade	Very Hard	Medium	Hard	Medium

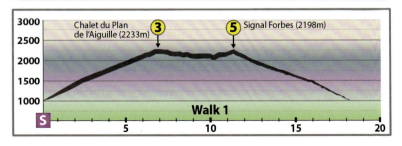

Chalet du Plan de l'Aiguille (2233m)

Signal Forbes (2198m)

Walk 1

Mer de Glace: the Connoisseur's Route

Everybody wants to see the famous Mer de Glace

This is one of the finest walks in the Alps and is a Chamonix classic. Everyone who visits the Chamonix Valley wants to see the famous Mer de Glace and this walk takes you to Signal Forbes, the finest viewpoint from which to gaze at it. Although the glacier has receded substantially in recent years, it is undeniably impressive and is overlooked by a host of magnificent peaks. After descending from Signal Forbes, you will reach Montenvers where most people go to view the glacier.

However, there is more to this route than the Mer de Glace. You will also walk the incredible balcony path between Plan de l'Aiguille and Montenvers which is known as the 'Grand Balcon Nord': the scenery is exquisite as you pass just below a variety of peaks and glaciers. The views over to the W side of the valley are also exceptional and the balcony is a much more peaceful place than Montenvers.

This walk's delights are not given away cheaply though: the initial climb from the valley floor is long and hard. However, towards the top, as you approach Chalet du Plan de l'Aiguille, the exertions will be forgotten when you see the magnificent views of MB.

Start/Finish: Car park for the Aiguille du Midi cable car in Chamonix, which is just beside the D1506 road: ///barrel.yeast.fern. You can walk to the start from Chamonix's main street: head for the lower station of the Aiguille du Midi cable car. Pass to the left of the cable car station, heading SE. Just afterwards, head through a tunnel under the D1506 and just afterwards, arrive at the car park.

Public Transport: Bus lines V1, V2 and 3, and the Mulet, all stop at the car park. Bus lines 1, 2, 3, V1 and V2 all stop at Chamonix Sud (which is near the lower station of the Aiguille du Midi cable car) and Chamonix Centre. There are train stations near Aiguille du Midi and Chamonix town centre.

Food/Drink: Chalet du Plan de l'Aiguille; Restaurants at Montenvers

Map: 3630OT Chamonix

Montenvers is linked to Chamonix by tramway so it can be very busy. The attractions there include the Ice Cave, a crystal gallery, a souvenir shop and places to eat: the huge open terrace of the restaurant is spectacular.

The route uses clear paths throughout, and there are plenty of signposts, so navigation is generally straightforward. Nevertheless, take care following the signposts on the descent from Montenvers as there are a number of different paths.

This walk is long and challenging: there is a lot of climbing and descent. However, you could shorten it in a variety of ways:

Variant A: to avoid the tough climb, you can use the Aiguille du Midi cable car to ascend to Plan de l'Aiguille: exit the cable car at the first stop (2310m). Then descend N on a path to Chalet du Plan de l'Aiguille (10-15min) (Waypoint No.3).

Variant B: to avoid the long descent from Montenvers, you can catch the Montenvers Tramway from Waypoint No.6 to head back to Chamonix.

Variant C: you can avoid both the climb to Chalet du Plan de l'Aiguille and the descent from Montenvers by using the Aiguille du Midi cable car (see Variant A) and the Montenvers Tramway (see Variant B).

The Grand Balcon Nord

Chalet du Plan de l'Aiguille

1

S See Map 1 (red route line). From the NE corner of the car park, pick up a path ('Plan de l'Aiguille').

1 0:20: At a junction, bear left and climb on a path. At any junctions, follow signs for 'Plan de l'Aiguille'.

2 1:20: TR at a faint junction (pink writing on a rock): easy to miss.

3 3:30: Arrive at **Chalet du Plan de l'Aiguille (2233m)**. Now follow the Grand Balcon Nord, contouring around the hillside generally NE. At any junctions, follow signs for 'Montenvers/Mer de Glace'.

4 5:00: TR at a fork and climb: note that both directions are signed to 'Montenvers/ Mer de Glace'.

5 5:30: Arrive at the signpost at **Signal Forbes (2198m)**: TR, leaving the main path. A few minutes later, reach an incredible viewpoint over the Mer de Glace. When you can drag yourself away, return to the signpost: TR and descend. Just before Montenvers, the path splinters: head towards the hotel.

6 6:15: Arrive at the hotel at **Montenvers (1913m)**: from there, you can visit the attractions, including another incredible viewpoint over the Mer de Glace. At the Chamonix Valley side of the hotel, pick up a path descending alongside the tram tracks. Soon, keep SH, ignoring a faint path on the right (which is signposted to 'Rochers des Mottets'). A few minutes later, TL at a junction ('Chamonix par Caillet').

7 6:35: Cross the tram tracks and descend on a path.

8 6:55: Keep SH past **Buvette le Caillet (1590m)**, still descending.

9 7:35: Cross the tram tracks and continue on a path on the other side. Now at junctions, follow signs for 'Chamonix'. Keep SH through the 'Parc Aventure' near les Mouilles. Shortly afterwards, TL and descend on a road. Soon afterwards, cross the tracks beside the lower station of the Montenvers Tramway. Then TL and walk just to the right of the station. Shortly, at a junction, TR and cross a bridge to head into the centre of Chamonix. Alternatively, keep SH to return to the Aiguille du Midi car park.

F 8:00: Arrive in the centre of **Chamonix (1037m)**.

2

	Main Route	Variant A
Time	7:30	6:00
Distance	17.2km 10.7 miles	13.2km 8.2 miles
Ascent	1618m 5309ft	1268m 4160ft
Descent	1618m 5309ft	1268m 4160ft
Maximum Altitude	2589m 8495ft	2589m 8495ft
Grade	Very Hard	Hard

Glacier de Taconnaz

6 la Jonction (2589m)

Walk 2

S

La Jonction

Admiring the Aiguilles Rouges

This challenging route is another Chamonix Valley classic. It involves a long climb and then a long descent by the same route. It may be tiring but the scenery is exquisite: if you want to get close to a glacier, then this is the walk for you. The goal of the route is the exceptional viewpoint known simply as 'la Jonction' which is only a few metres away from Glacier des Bossons. However, all the way up (and down) there are incredible views of both Glacier des Bossons and Glacier de Taconnaz which are directly underneath the summit of MB itself. The slopes are covered with Alpenrose which is a vibrant pink colour in early summer.

The large altitude gain and loss make the route very challenging. The paths are mostly clear and easy to follow so navigation is largely straightforward. However, at times the route is rocky and steep. There are also a few sections where you must scramble up the rocks: take care to follow the waymarks and watch your footing. Snow can lie on this route until early summer. Start early to avoid climbing in the heat.

Warning: do not walk on the glacier. If you fall into a crevice, it is unlikely that you would ever be recovered.

Variant A: Shorten the route by ascending and descending part of the way using Télésiège du Glacier des Bossons. The upper station of the chair-lift is at 1400m (Waypoint No.2) so this reduces the climb and descent by around 350m.

Start/Finish: The car park at the lower station of Télésiège du Glacier des Bossons, near les Bossons: ///resets.upsetting.themselves. Alternatively, you can park higher up at the hamlet of le Mont (Waypoint No.1).

Public Transport: Bus line 2 connects Télésiège du Glacier des Bossons with les Bossons, Chamonix, les Praz, Argentière and le Tour. The nearest train station is at les Bossons: from there, you can walk to the start point (15-20min) or catch bus line 2.

Food/Drink: Chalet du Glacier des Bossons; Chalet des Pyramides; Restaurant beside the car park

Map: 3531ET St-Gervais-les-Bains

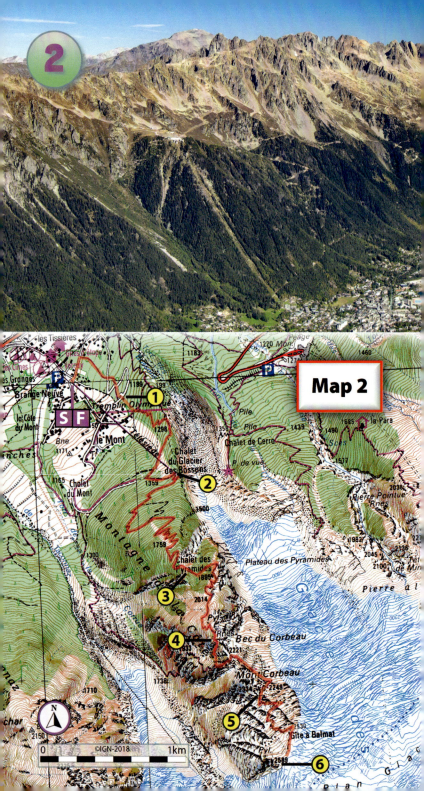

Wonderful views of the Chamonix Valley from la Jonction

S See Map 2. Head N on 'Route du Tremplin'. A few minutes later, TR on a path (yellow sign) and climb through trees. Soon, cross a road and continue upwards on a path. When you reach the road again, continue uphill on a tarmac lane.

(1) 0:20: Shortly, at the parking area at **le Mont**, cross the road a third time: continue uphill on a path ('la Jonction'). Now climb through the forest, following signposts for 'la Jonction': keep on the main path, ignoring offshoots.

(2) 1:00: Continue upwards past the top of the chair-lift. A few minutes later, arrive at a junction: TL to stop at the lovely **Chalet du Glacier des Bossons (1425m)**. Otherwise, TR to continue upwards on the route. Just afterwards, TR at another junction.

(3) 2:30: Reach a superb viewpoint of Glacier de Taconnaz. Just afterwards, descend steeply on wooden steps, protected with a cable. Soon, climb again and Glacier des Bossons comes into view. Pass **Chalet des Pyramides (1895m)**. Just afterwards, TR at a junction: do not descend to the left.

(4) 3:15: Keep SH at a wonderful viewpoint overlooking Glacier de Taconnaz and continue on a magnificent balcony path, now descending. 5min later, climb again. When you head over a spur and go around a corner, Glacier des Bossons appears again: the incredible path heads directly towards it. 5-10min later, TR at a junction, following yellow waymarks up through rock: the path to the left would take you to a magnificent viewpoint right beside the glacier. Soon, there is a short section of metal railings and steps.

(5) 3:45: Keep SH at a junction beside a cairn (yellow waymarks). Soon, climb steeply through more sections of rocks. Pass **Gîte à Balmat** which was used by Jacques Balmat and Michel Paccard during the first ascent of Mont Blanc in 1786.

(6) 4:30: Climb a granite slab to arrive at **la Jonction (2589m)**, a stunning viewpoint a few metres away from the glacier. Retrace your steps downwards.

F 7:30: Arrive back at the start.

3

	Main Route	Variant A
Time	6:30	3:45
Distance	15.8km 9.8 miles	10.5km 6.5 miles
Ascent	1100m 3609ft	472m 1549ft
Descent	1100m 3609ft	1050m 3445ft
Maximum Altitude	2372m 7783ft	2372m 7783ft
Grade	Hard	Medium

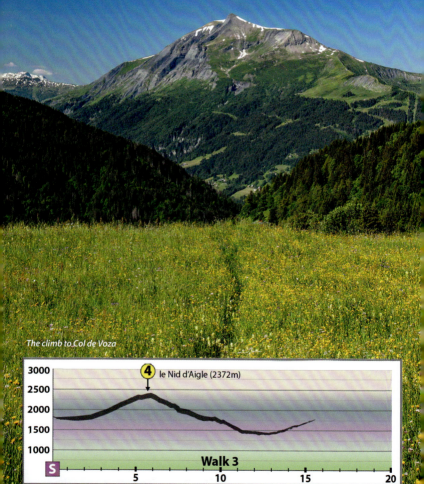

The climb to Col de Voza

4 le Nid d'Aigle (2372m)

Walk 3

Le Nid d'Aigle

3

The incredible views at Col de Voza

A wonderful route climbing through pastures decked with wild-flowers to a superb refuge overlooking Glacier de Bionnassay: the spectacular terrace is a great place for lunch. You can also walk right up to the glacier if you have a little energy to spare. The second half of the route descends all the way to the hamlet of le Crozat via a thrilling suspension bridge across a raging torrent. Another climb rounds things off, offering sublime views of the Glacier and Aiguille de Bionnassay.

T he route mostly uses clear paths which are easy to follow. However, there is a tricky section at Waypoint No.3: it is very steep and there are metal steps and cables to assist so take great care. The descent through forest, after Waypoint No.6, is confusing: look out for the yellow signs. This section is steep too.

> **Variant A:** to avoid the climb to Nid d'Aigle, you can use the Tramway du Mont Blanc. Just follow the walk directions until you reach the tram's track and station. From there, the tramway takes you all the way to Waypoint No.4.

Start/Finish: The lower station of the Bellevue cable car in les Houches: ///livened.anyhow.appraisals

Public Transport: The route takes advantage of the Bellevue cable car to ascend and descend. Bus lines 1 and V1 connect the cable car with les Houches, la Griaz and Chamonix. Bus line 1 also continues to les Praz. The nearest train station (les Houches) is near la Griaz, from where you can catch bus lines 1 or V1 to the Bellevue cable car: alternatively it is a 15-20min walk.

Food/Drink: Refuge de Nid d'Aigle; Col de Voza; les Houches

Map: 3531ET St-Gervais-les-Bains

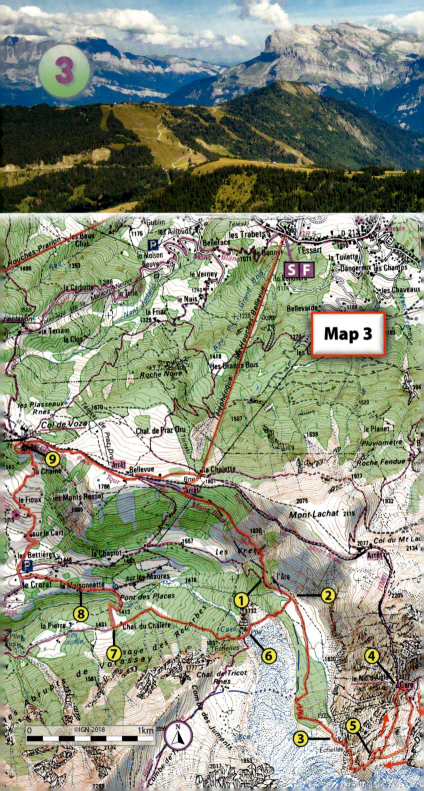

Col de Voza and le Prarion (Walk 4) viewed from near le Nid d'Aigle

S See Map 3. Ascend in the Bellevue cable car to the upper station at **la Chalette (1794m)**. Keep SH out of the station ('Nid d'Aigle'). Shortly afterwards, descend and cross the tracks of the Tramway du Mont Blanc. Then continue descending on a path. A few minutes later, TL on a broad path ('Nid d'Aigle') which undulates, never losing or gaining much height. The path is narrow and there are some short sections of rocks to climb: occasionally there are cables fixed into the rocks to assist.

(1) 0:25: Keep SH at a junction ('Nid d'Aigle').

(2) 0:30: 5min later, keep SH at a junction at **Plat de l'Are (1775m)**. 5-10min later, start to climb.

(3) 1:15: Just after crossing a stream, the gradient increases: there are some metal steps and cables to assist. There are good views down into the rocky moraine of Glacier de Bionnassay. Further up, the views of the glacier itself are awesome.

(4) 2:45: TR at le **Nid d'Aigle (2372m)**, the upper station for the Tramway du Mont Blanc. 5min later, arrive at Refuge de Nid d'Aigle. Head S on a path directly towards Glacier de Bionnassay. Shortly afterwards, TR at a fork (large cairn): if you wish to get closer to the glacier then you could take the path on the left. Shortly afterwards, TR at another fork and descend SW down a grassy spur.

(5) 3:15: Re-join the path travelled earlier and retrace your steps downwards.

(2) 4:15: TL at the junction passed earlier at **Plat de l'Are (1775m)** ('le Crozat'). Climb briefly and then descend steeply.

(6) 4:25: Cross a suspension bridge over a torrent and then climb. A few minutes later, TR at a junction ('le Crozat') and descend steeply through trees: there are some metal steps and railings to assist. Cross a forest track and continue on a path on the other side. Shortly afterwards, cross the track again (yellow sign) and pick up the path on the other side. Now simply follow the yellow signs.

(7) 4:55: TR at a junction just after a chalet ('le Crozat'). 5min later, cross a bridge and then climb briefly. Shortly afterwards, keep SH at a junction ('le Crozat').

(8) 5:10: TR at a junction beside a chalet ('Col de Voza'). 10min later, follow a road through a hamlet. A few minutes later, TR onto a road ('Col de Voza'). Shortly afterwards, keep SH at a junction, remaining on the road. Shortly after that, keep SH climbing on a track ('Col de Voza').

(9) 6:10: Arrive at **Col de Voza (1653m)**: TR just before crossing the tram tracks ('Bellevue') and follow a path alongside them. 10-15min later, bear left just after a building and cross the tracks. Just afterwards, TR at a junction. 5min later, arrive back at the upper station of the Bellevue cable car. Descend in the cable car to return to the start.

4

Time	3:30
Distance	8.5km 5.3 miles
Ascent	157m 515ft
Descent	989m 3245ft
Maximum Altitude	1969m 6460ft
Grade	Medium

Le Prarion
alt. 1969 m

Télécabine Les Houches-Prarion   0h15
Hôtel du Prarion   0h20
La Charme   0h40
Bionnassay   1h45

Col de la Forclaz   0h50

① le Prarion (1969m)   les Houches (1012m)   F

3000
2500
2000
1500
1000

Walk 4

S   5   10

Le Prarion

4

Charousse has a spectacular setting

The summit of le Prarion is the destination of this spectacular walk. For the Chamonix Valley, the height of this outlying peak is relatively small but the views from it are anything but. In fact, it is perhaps the finest place of all from which to view the entire MB Massif. Because it is set back slightly from the principal peaks, it is a superlative vantage point from which to get an overall perspective of the massif: MB and its neighbours are on full display. On a clear day, you will want to spend some time on the summit to identify all the peaks of the range. As a bonus, the descent passes the lovely hamlet of Charousse which has the MB Massif as its spectacular backdrop. This is not a walk to be missed.

As the route takes advantage of the Prarion cable car to gain altitude, it is only a short climb to the summit. The descent is long though. If you prefer climbing rather than descending then you could walk it in reverse, descending using the cable car.

The path on the descent from the summit is steep, narrow and exposed in places. There are also some short sections of rocks to descend: take care.

Start/Finish: The lower station of the Prarion cable car in les Houches: ///library.ordered.penalties

Public Transport: The route uses the Prarion cable car to ascend. Bus lines 1 and V1 connect the cable car with les Houches, la Griaz and Chamonix. Bus line 1 also continues to les Praz. The nearest train station (les Houches) is near la Griaz, from where you can catch bus lines 1 or V1 to the Prarion cable car: alternatively it is a 15-20min walk.

Food/Drink: Le Prarion Hotel-Restaurant near the upper station of the Prarion cable car; les Houches

Map: 3531ET St-Gervais-les-Bains

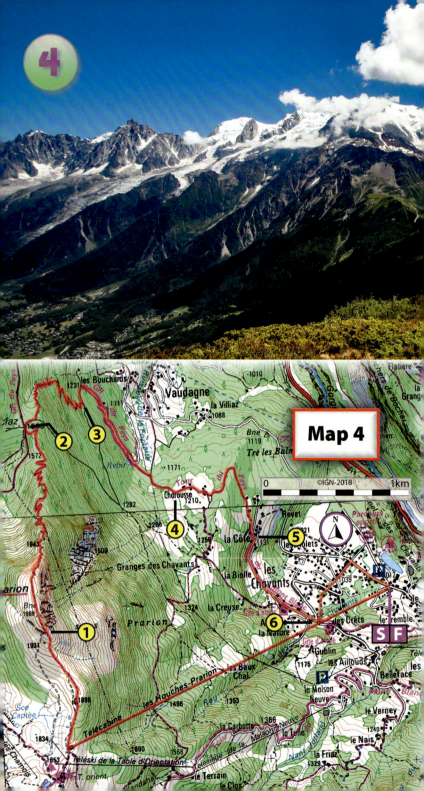

The MB Massif viewed from le Prarion

S See Map 4. Ascend using the Prarion cable car to the **upper station (1853m)**. Just after leaving the station, TR on a path climbing N ('le Prarion'). Shortly afterwards, TR and head across a section of gravel: on the other side, pick up the path again (yellow waymark).

1 0:30: Climb a steep, rocky section. A few minutes later, reach the summit of l**e Prarion (1969m)**: there is an excellent orientation table enabling identification of all the visible peaks. Continue N along the summit ridge and soon start to descend steeply.

2 1:40: TR at **Col de la Forclaz (1533m)**. Shortly afterwards, TR at another junction ('les Houches'). Shortly after that, TL at another junction ('Charousse'): initially, the gradient is gentle but it becomes steeper.

3 2:10: TL onto a track and continue descending. 10min later, TR onto a path ('Charousse'). A few minutes later, TR onto another path and climb for 5min.

4 2:35: Arrive in **Charousse (1210m)**: follow a broad path through the middle of the magnificent hamlet. Afterwards, keep SH on a track ('les Houches').

5 3:00: At a junction, keep SH, descending on a road ('les Houches'). TR at the next junction, still on the road (yellow sign).

6 3:15: At a road junction, bear left and cross over to a path heading downhill ('les Houches'). The path becomes a lane, descending between houses. Soon, cross over a road and continue downhill. Cross another road and continue downhill. At the next junction, TR and walk along 'Route des Chavants'.

F 3:30: A few minutes later, arrive back at the lower station of the Prarion cable car.

5

Time	6:30
Distance	13.2km 8.2 miles
Ascent	1040m 3412ft
Descent	1040m 3412ft
Maximum Altitude	2285m 7497ft
Grade	Hard

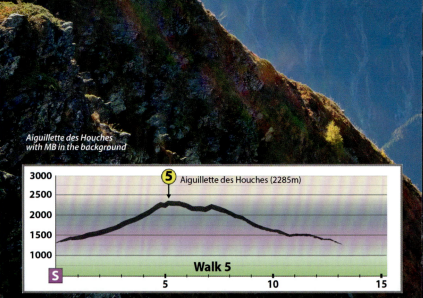

Aiguillette des Houches with MB in the background

5 Aiguillette des Houches (2285m)

Walk 5

S

Aiguillette des Houches

Views of the MB Massif on the descent

The walk starts in aromatic forest and then climbs an incredible ridge to Aiguillette des Houches. From the ridge and summit, the views are exceptional: both face the MB Massif to the SE and the landscape to the N is wonderful too. After the summit, there is a long traverse through spectacular pastures and the panorama at Refuge Bellachat is sublime: lunch on the terrace is an unforgettable experience.

The route uses clear paths which are generally well marked so navigation is usually straightforward. However, after Refuge Bellachat there are a variety of paths to choose from so follow signs and waymarks closely. The descent from the refuge is very steep in places.

Start/Finish: The small parking area at le Bettey (1352m): ///contrived.purport.relaying

Public Transport: This is the only walk in this book where the public transport is a little inconvenient. That said, access by bus/train is perfectly possible if you do not mind some extra climbing. The nearest bus stop is at la Griaz: it is a 1hr climb on foot from there to le Bettey. Bus lines 1 and V1 connect la Griaz with Chamonix: bus line 1 also continues to les Praz. The nearest train station (les Houches) is near la Griaz.

Food/Drink: Refuge Bellachat

Map: 3531ET St-Gervais-les-Bains

An incredible October day at Aiguillette des Houches

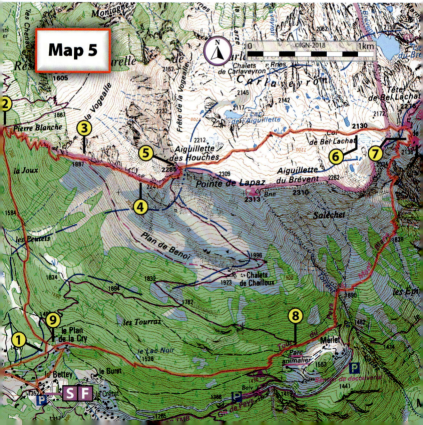

S See Map 5. From the parking area, walk up the road. Shortly afterwards, ignore a path on the right. When the road ends, TR onto a track ('Aiguillette des Houches'). Shortly afterwards, TR at a fork ('Aiguillette des Houches').

1 0:15: TL at a junction. Shortly afterwards, TL at a fork. Now at junctions follow signs for 'Pierre Blanche'.

2 0:50: TR at the junction at **Pierre Blanche (1697m)**. Soon the path narrows and starts to climb more steeply.

3 1:40: Keep SH at a junction, still climbing ('Aiguillette des Houches').

4 2:30: Keep SH on a path which runs to the right of the ridge. Soon, keep SH at a junction and zigzag upwards.

5 3:00: TL at a little saddle. A few metres later, reach the summit of **Aiguillette des Houches (2285m)**. Return to the saddle and keep SH on a magnificent path snaking across the grassy slopes, to the left of the ridge.

6 3:40: Just after a cairn, TR at a fork, remaining on the main path. 10min later, keep SH at a junction ('les Houches').

7 3:55: Arrive at **Refuge Bellachat (2136m)**. Head S from the refuge. Just afterwards, keep SH at a junction ('les Houches') and start the long descent.

8 5:30: TL at a junction ('le Christ Roi'). 10min later, TR at another junction ('le Bettey'). Now at any junctions, follow signs for 'le Bettey'.

9 6:15: TL at a junction ('le Bettey') and pass just to the right of a beautiful chalet. Shortly afterwards, pick up a path heading downhill between a stone wall and a wooden building. Shortly afterwards, TR at a junction onto a narrow path, still descending. A few minutes later, TR on a track. After a few minutes more, TL down some steps ('le Bettey').

F 6:30: TL onto the road and soon arrive back at the start.

Map 6

6

Time	3:30
Distance	8.8km 5.5 miles
Ascent	15m 49ft
Descent	1453m 4767ft
Maximum Altitude	2525m 8285ft
Grade	Medium

The cable car station on the summit of le Brévent

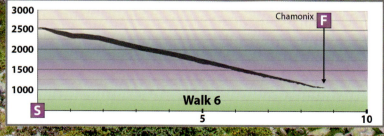

Chamonix **F**

3000
2500
2000
1500
1000

Walk 6

S   5   10

The Mont Blanc Balcony

6

Refuge Bellachat

This magnificent walk is a highlight of the Chamonix Valley. The summit of le Brévent (where you start walking) is one of the most famous viewpoints for MB. Furthermore, the path from le Brévent to Refuge Bellachat is an epic balcony through rock and pastures with stupendous views of the MB Massif. The panorama from the terrace of Refuge Bellachat is also sublime and a break there is an unforgettable experience.

Given the high quality of the scenery, it is no surprise that the area around le Brévent is a 'honey pot' which attracts large crowds in peak season. However, if you arrive early in the day then you should find it to be relatively peaceful. The route uses clear paths and navigation is straightforward. The descent is a long 'knee-jerker' though! In some years, snow lies near le Brévent until early July so take care.

Variant A: Walk 6 can be combined with Walk 7. See Variant A of Walk 7.

Variant B: Walk 6 can be combined with both Walks 7 and 11 for a truly epic day out. See Variant B of Walk 7.

Start/Finish: The lower station of the Planpraz cable car in Chamonix: ///jiggle.stylings.name

Public Transport: The walk uses the Planpraz/Brévent cable cars to ascend. Chamonix Centre is the nearest bus stop: from there, it is a short walk to the cable car station. Bus lines 1, 2, 3, V1 and V2 all stop at Chamonix Centre. There are train stations near Aiguille du Midi and Chamonix town centre, both of which are a short walk from the cable car station.

Food/Drink: le Brévent; Refuge Bellachat; Chamonix

Map: 3531ET St-Gervais-les-Bains and 3630OT Chamonix

The rocky descent from le Brévent

S See Map 6 (red route line). Ascend to Planpraz by cable car. Then change onto the cable car for le Brévent. From **le Brévent (2525m)**, head downhill on a wide path. Soon, TL at a junction ('Bellachat'), descending on a rocky path which is tricky to follow in places: watch for waymarks. After a short descent, the gradient eases and the path makes a stunning traverse around the hillside. After a while, start to descend more steeply.

1 1:15: TL at a signpost ('Chamonix') beside **Refuge Bellachat (2136m)**, descending steeply towards the Chamonix Valley.

2 2:20: TR at the junction at Plan de Bel Lachat. 20min later, TL at another junction ('Chamonix'). Afterwards, stay on the main path, ignoring smaller offshoots.

3 3:00: Shortly after crossing a stream, bear left to arrive at a junction: TR ('Chamonix'), still descending. 5min later, TR at a fork ('Chamonix'). Just afterwards, keep SH, ignoring another path on the right. A few minutes later, cross over a track and continue descending on a path on the other side ('Chamonix'). Keep SH, crossing a few small roads.

4 3:15: At the hamlet of **les Moettieux**, TL onto a road and descend. 5min later, TL at a junction. Keep SH at the next junction, ignoring a signpost directing you right for Chamonix town centre.

F 3:30: Arrive back at the lower station of the **Planpraz cable car (1087m)**.

MB seen from the incredible balcony on Walk 6

Soaking in the views of MB on the climb to the col

7

	Main Route	Variant A	Variant B	Variant C
Time	1:45	5:15	7:00	3:30
Distance	3.0km 1.9 miles	11.8km 7.3 miles	16.6km 10.6 miles	7.8km 5.1 miles
Ascent	555m 1821ft	570m 1870ft	788m 2585ft	773m 2536ft
Descent	30m 98ft	1483m 4866ft	1579m 5181ft	126m 413ft
Maximum Altitude	2525m 8285ft	2525m 8285ft	2525m 8285ft	2525m 8285ft
Grade	Medium	Hard	Very Hard	Hard

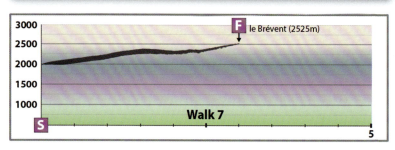

le Brévent (2525m)

Walk 7

Col du Brévent

7

Climbing to Col du Brévent

This walk may be short but it packs a punch: the views of MB all the way are spectacular and le Brévent itself (where you finish walking) is one of the most famous MB viewpoints of all. Col du Brévent is a fabulous place too with incredible views to the N adding to those of the MB Massif to the S. The terrain between the col and le Brévent is wonderfully wild.

The climb to le Brévent may be steep in places but the path is generally good. However, in some years snow lies until early July so take care: navigation between Col du Brévent and le Brévent is tricky in snowy conditions. Before le Brévent there is a steep climb up rocks with a short section of metal ladders to assist: these are best avoided if you have a fear of heights.

Variant A: Walk 7 can be combined with Walk 6 making a longer route from Planpraz to Chamonix (via le Brévent). For this option, follow Walk 7 to le Brévent: from there, follow the Walk 6 directions.

Variant B: Walk 7 can be combined with both Walks 6 and 11 for a truly epic day out. For this option, take the cable car to la Flégère and follow Walk 11 to la Parsa cable car station near Planpraz: from there, follow Walk 7 to le Brévent. From le Brévent, follow Walk 6 to Chamonix.

Variant C: Walk 7 can be combined with Walk 11 making a superb route from la Flégère to le Brévent (via Planpraz). For this option, take the cable car to la Flégère and follow Walk 11 to la Parsa cable car station near Planpraz: from there, follow Walk 7 to le Brévent. From le Brévent, descend in the cable car to Chamonix.

Start/Finish: The lower station of the Planpraz cable car in Chamonix: ///jiggle.stylings.name

Public Transport: This walk uses the Planpraz cable car to ascend and the Brévent and Planpraz cable cars to descend. Chamonix Centre is the nearest bus stop: from there, it is a short walk to the cable car station. Bus lines 1, 2, 3, V1 and V2 all stop at Chamonix Centre. There are train stations near Aiguille du Midi and Chamonix town centre, both of which are a short walk from the cable car station.

Food/Drink: Planpraz; le Brévent; Chamonix

Map: 3630OT Chamonix

The scenery changes after Col du Brévent

S See Map 6 (blue route line). Ascend to **Planpraz (1999m)** by cable car. Climb NW on a track. 5-10min later, arrive at the top of **'la Parsa' ski-lift (2075m)**. From there, climb NW on a small path ('Col du Brévent').

1 0:20: TL at a **junction (2197m)** and climb SW on a path.

2 1:00: TL at **Col du Brévent (2368m)** and follow a marked path which zigzags up a ridge. A few minutes later, the path drifts to the right of the ridge (yellow waymarks). Soon the path heads down the right side of a broad gully. Eventually, the path leaves the gully and then climbs again (waymarks/cairns). 5-10min later, scramble up a short section of rocks and then climb some metal ladders fixed into the rocks: take care. The ladders are best avoided if you have a fear of heights. Afterwards, continue climbing on a clear path. A few minutes later, follow waymarks up over rocks.

3 1:30: TR at a large cairn and climb more gently up a track.

4 1:40: Keep SH at a junction, still climbing. 5min later, arrive at **le Brévent (2525m)**. Now descend to Chamonix using the Brévent and Planpraz cable cars.

The final climb to le Brévent

7

8

Time	3:30
Distance	7.0km 4.4 miles
Ascent	553m 1814ft
Descent	553m 1814ft
Maximum Altitude	2414m 7920ft
Grade	Hard

Climbing to Col du Lac Cornu

Lac Cornu (2276m)

Walk 8

Lac Cornu

The view from near
Col du Lac Cornu

8

A stunning walk to the sublime Lac Cornu, one of the Chamonix Valley's more peaceful places: most people tend to view the lake from Col du Lac Cornu and do not make the effort to negotiate the rocky path to the lake itself. Although it is true that the view from the col is spectacular, it is lovely to picnic on the rocks on the N side of the lake.

The beautiful views are not given away cheaply though. The climb to Col du Lac Cornu is steep in places. Furthermore, the path between the col and Lac Cornu heads through rocky terrain and is occasionally hard to follow. The final section towards the N tip of Lac Cornu is particularly difficult. In some years, snow lies near the col and lake until early July so take care: navigation to the lake is tricky in snowy conditions. Avoid this walk in poor weather or low visibility.

Start/Finish: The lower station of the Planpraz cable car in Chamonix: ///jiggle.stylings.name

Public Transport: This walk uses the Planpraz cable car to ascend and descend. Chamonix Centre is the nearest bus stop: from there, it is a short walk to the cable car station. Bus lines 1, 2, 3, V1 and V2 all stop at Chamonix Centre. There are train stations near Aiguille du Midi and Chamonix town centre, both of which are a short walk from the cable car station.

Food/Drink: Planpraz; Chamonix

Map: 3630OT Chamonix

S See Map 6 (green route line). Ascend to **Planpraz (1999m)** by cable car. Climb NW on a track. 5-10min later, arrive at the top of **'la Parsa' ski-lift (2075m)**. From there, head N on a path ('Lac Cornu').

1 0:15: After a few minutes, TL onto a path which soon climbs as it contours around the slopes. After a while, zigzag steeply upwards to the N.

2 1:35: Arrive at **Col du Lac Cornu (2414m)**. Bear left and head NW on a faint path ('Lac Cornu') towards the lake which is visible below. This path through rocky terrain heads around the right side of the lake to its N tip: take care as it is hard to follow in places.

3 2:00: Reach the N tip of **Lac Cornu (2276m)**. Now retrace your steps back to the upper station of the Planpraz cable car: use the lift to descend to Chamonix.

Lac Cornu

8

Time	3:00
Distance	9.9km 6.2 miles
Ascent	105m 345ft
Descent	105m 345ft
Maximum Altitude	1084m 3557ft
Grade	Easy

The River l'Arve at les Tines

les Tines (1082m)

Walk 9

3000
2500
2000
1500
1000

S

5   10

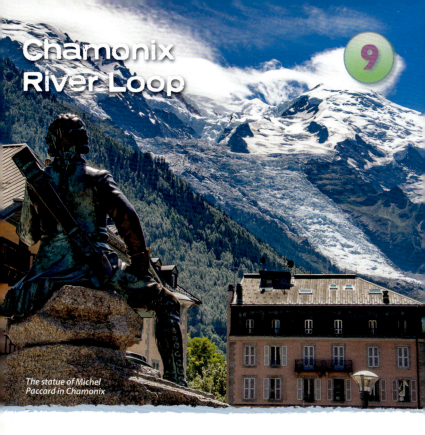

Chamonix River Loop

9

The statue of Michel Paccard in Chamonix

This beautiful valley walk takes place at lower altitudes but that does not mean it is lacking in incredible views. A host of famous peaks are on view including the mighty MB itself. It is a great option if the weather looks unsettled, you only have half a day to spare or you want an easier day after previously completing some more difficult walks. Because the route enters Chamonix itself, it is lovely to combine it with an exploration session around the town: relax and have a meal or a drink at the end.

Navigation is occasionally fiddly so follow the directions closely. The route uses good paths and tracks throughout. Because of the relatively low altitude, the walk can be undertaken at most times of year.

Start/Finish: The fountain in 'Place Jacques Balmat' in Chamonix town centre: ///forming.relaunch.speaker

Public Transport: Bus lines 1, 2, 3, V1 and V2 all stop at Chamonix Centre. There are train stations near Aiguille du Midi and Chamonix town centre.

Food/Drink: Chamonix; Hotel Arveyron; Buvette du Paradis des Praz; les Praz de Chamonix

Map: 3630OT Chamonix

Map 7

Summer flowers in Chamonix

S See Map 7 (orange route line). From the fountain in 'Place Jacques Balmat', head SE. Shortly, TL after the statue of Saussure. Shortly afterwards, TR at the statue of Paccard (see page 75). Take the next left onto 'Rue Whymper'. Soon keep SH across a roundabout. At the next roundabout, TL. Just afterwards, TR on a path which heads NE alongside the road.

1 0:20: Soon afterwards, TL at a fork on a gravel path and enter a forest park known as 'Bois du Bouchet'. A few minutes later, TL at a fork. Cross a grassy plain with beautiful views of les Drus up ahead and MB behind. Keep SH across a tarmac lane.

2 0:45: TR at a fork and head through tunnels under the road and railway. Just afterwards, at Hotel Arveyron, TR at a fork on a tarmac lane. After a while, when you leave the trees, the views open up: the whole W side of the Chamonix Valley is visible, including le Brévent and the Aiguilles Rouges. Soon, keep SH at a junction beside a bridge ('Montenvers').

3 1:10: Ignore a path heading upwards on the right and keep SH on the track. Shortly afterwards, TL at a fork. Soon, TL and cross a bridge. Immediately afterwards, take the middle of three paths. At the next junction, TR across a tarmac platform used for shooting ('les Praz'). Keep SH at the next junction. Shortly afterwards, TR onto a small road, 'Chemin de la Source de l'Arveyron'. A few minutes later, ignore a path on the left and continue up the road. When the road ends, bear left on a path. Immediately afterwards, TL at a fork and climb. A few minutes later, TL onto another path ('Grand Balcon Nord').

4 1:30: TL at a junction: at the date of press, the signpost here was misleading. Shortly afterwards, keep SH, ignoring a path on the right. 5-10min later, keep SH, descending on a small road.

5 1:45: TL onto the road at **les Tines (1082m)**. Just afterwards, TR and pass through some gates at the railway station. Cross the tracks and TR on 'Chemin de la Tannerie'. Shortly afterwards, TL onto 'Chemin du Martinet'. A few minutes later, cross a footbridge over the River l'Arve. Immediately afterwards, TL and walk on a broad path through the trees, alongside the river. Soon, TR at a fork. 5min later, keep SH past Buvette du Paradis des Praz.

6 2:05: Cross a footbridge over the River l'Arve. Immediately afterwards, TR on a path. A few minutes later, keep SH through the grounds of Hotel le Labrador. TR and walk on a footpath alongside the main road. A few minutes later, when the road bends left, keep SH on a path. A few minutes later, pass the chapel in **les Praz de Chamonix (1056m)**. Soon the road (now 'Route des Praz') bends right. Just before a bridge, TL onto a path running down the left bank of the river ('Chamonix').

7 2:45: Bear left, cross two footbridges and then TR onto another path ('Chamonix Centre').

8 3:00: Cross a road and bear right onto a footpath to head back into Chamonix.

Time	2:15
Distance	5.8km 3.6 miles
Ascent	315m 1034ft
Descent	315m 1034ft
Maximum Altitude	1367m 4485ft
Grade	Easy

The views through gaps in the trees from the 'Petit Balcon Sud'

S See Map 7 (blue route line). From the car park, head S back to the main road: TR and walk along 'Route des Praz' through the village of les Praz. Shortly after crossing a bridge over the River l'Arve, TR and climb on a path ('la Floria'). A few minutes later, TL at a junction ('la Floria').

1 0:30: TR at a junction ('la Floria'). Shortly afterwards, TL at a fork ('la Floria').

2 1:00: Arrive at **Chalet de la Floria (1337m)**. Afterwards, the path heads NE. There are beautiful views of MB through gaps in the trees. 5-10min later, TR at a junction ('les Praz'), heading steeply downhill. After 5min, TR and descend on a track. Shortly afterwards, TR onto a narrow path, zigzagging down the slope. The path crosses the track a few times: keep following the path directly downhill towards the valley floor and keep downhill at any junctions.

3 1:30: When you arrive at a wider path, TR onto it: this is the 'Petit Balcon Sud'. Keep SH at a junction.

1 2:00: Shortly afterwards, arrive back at Waypoint No.1: TL and retrace your steps to the start.

2 Chalet de la Floria (1337m)

Walk 10

Chalet de la Floria

Fabulous views of MB from Chalet de la Floria

This route may be short but it is still wonderful. The pretty, flower-decked buvette at la Floria enables you to enjoy the magnificent views of MB and its glaciers at your leisure with a drink or something to eat. The village of les Praz also has some restaurants and cafes for a drink at the end.

The route uses good paths throughout and navigation is straightforward. There are shorter routes between la Floria and les Praz but we have opted for the slightly longer (but prettier) return journey along the 'Petit Balcon Sud' which offers tantalising glimpses of MB through the trees. This walk is a super outing for a hot day as most of the climb is in the shade.

Start/Finish: The car park for the Flégère cable car, les Praz de Chamonix: ///lull.intention.pompom

Public Transport: Bus lines 1, 2 and V2 all stop at the start point in les Praz. There is a train station in les Praz which is a short walk from the start.

Food/Drink: Les Praz de Chamonix; Chalet de la Floria

Map: 3630OT Chamonix

11	

Time	1:45
Distance	5.2km 3.2 miles
Ascent	293m 961ft
Descent	171m 561ft
Maximum Altitude	2075m 6808ft
Grade	Medium

Mont Blanc is visible all the way on this epic walk

Walk 11

F Plan Praz cable car (1999m)

S

3000 2500 2000 1500 1000

5   10

Refuge la Flégère

Grand Balcon Sud: La Flégère to Planpraz

This walk is quite simply a delight and offers some of the Chamonix Valley's finest scenes, including exceptional views of MB. Straight away you will find yourself on a wonderful balcony path high above the valley floor, directly opposite the MB Massif. And you remain on the balcony, enjoying continuous views, all the way to Planpraz. This route is not to be missed.

The waymarking is sometimes poor so take extra care with navigation. Shortly after leaving la Flégère, there is a very steep section of steps: take care. Paths are mostly clear but there are a few rocky sections.

> **Variant A:** Walk 11 can be combined with both Walks 6 and 7 for a truly epic day out. See Variant B of Walk 7.
>
> **Variant B:** Walk 11 can be combined with Walk 7, making a superb route from la Flégère to le Brévent (via Planpraz). See Variant C of Walk 7.

Start/Finish: The walk takes advantage of the Flégère cable car to ascend. The car park for the lift is at les Praz de Chamonix: ///lull.intention.pompom. The walk uses the Planpraz cable car to descend so you finish near Chamonix town centre.

Public Transport: Bus lines 1, 2 and V2 all stop at the start point in les Praz. There is a train station in les Praz which is a short walk from the start. At the finish, bus lines 1, 2, 3, V1 and V2 all stop in Chamonix town centre. There are train stations near Aiguille du Midi and Chamonix town centre. If parking a car at the start in les Praz, you could use public transport to return to it at the end: alternatively, you could follow the directions for Walk 9 to walk back to les Praz.

Food/Drink: Les Praz de Chamonix; la Flégère; Planpraz; Chamonix

Map: 3630OT Chamonix

The epic balcony path offers incredible views of the MB Massif

S See Map 6 (orange route line). From the refuge at **la Flégère** (which is just below the cable car station), head SW on a path contouring around the hillside. After 5min, TL onto a track. Immediately afterwards, TR at a junction. Soon take care descending steep steps. Then climb gently over rocks and continue contouring around the hillside on an exquisite balcony.

1 0:50: Keep SH across a track and take a path heading S on the other side (poor waymarking). After 5min, keep SH at a junction.

2 1:00: TL onto a track. Immediately afterwards, TR onto a path contouring around the hillside: there are few waymarks so, at junctions, keep on the main path following cairns.

3 1:40: Arrive at the top of **'la Parsa' chairlift (2075m)**: TL at a junction and descend on a track. 5min later, arrive at the top of the **Planpraz cable car (1999m)**. Descend to Chamonix using the lift.

Sunset over MB viewed from Lac Blanc

	Main Route	Variant A
Time	3:15	2:30
Distance	6.5km 4.0 miles	6.5km 4.0 miles
Ascent	680m 2231ft	172m 564ft
Descent	172m 564ft	680m 2231ft
Maximum Altitude	2385m 7825ft	2385m 7825ft
Grade	Hard	Medium

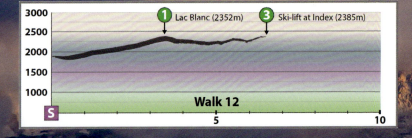

Lac Blanc (2352m)   **3** Ski-lift at Index (2385m)

Walk 12

Lac Blanc
(from la Flégère)

The views near Lac Blanc are unforgettable

Lac Blanc is another highlight of the Chamonix Valley and this is the most straightforward way of getting there. The reflection of the MB Massif in Lac Blanc on a fine day is a sight to behold. The balcony of the refuge beside the lake overlooks MB and is a superb place for lunch. When you can tear yourself away, you still have the long balcony path to the Index ski-lift to enjoy, looking straight at MB all the way.

As a side route, you can also explore the exceptional walking trail heading around the lake: it takes 20-30min. Watch for chamois and ibex between Lac Blanc and Index, especially early in the morning.

Sometimes snow lies on the route until early July, making navigation more difficult. In such conditions, the route can be slippery and a fall could be serious. Also, navigation can be difficult in bad weather or low visibility. The path to Lac Blanc is steep in places. Between Lac Blanc and Index, the undulating path is often rocky: there are a few sections where the path disappears and you need to follow waymarks.

> **Variant A:** the route can also be walked in reverse by ascending all the way to Waypoint No.3 by ski-lift and then walking to la Flégère. This option is easier as there is less uphill walking.

Start/Finish: This walk takes advantage of the Flégère cable car to ascend. The car park for the lift is at les Praz de Chamonix: ///lull.intention.pompom. The walk uses the Index and Flégère lifts to descend back to les Praz.

Public Transport: Bus lines 1, 2 and V2 all stop at the start point in les Praz. There is a train station in les Praz which is a short walk from the start.

Food/Drink: Les Praz de Chamonix; la Flégère; Refuge du Lac Blanc

Map: 3630OT Chamonix

S See Map 8 (green route line). Head N on a track and descend briefly to a plateau: TL at a junction on a broad path. A few minutes later, bear right, staying on the broad path. Soon, TL at a junction ('Lac Blanc') and start to climb more steeply. The path zigzags upwards and then contours (generally N) around the slopes. The views are exceptional. At any junctions, keep N, following signs for 'Lac Blanc'.

1 1:50: Arrive at **Refuge du Lac Blanc (2352m)** with its incredible setting beside Lac Blanc. From the refuge, retrace your steps S ('Index'). After 10min, TR at a junction ('Index'). Now a superb balcony path contours around the slopes. Later, ignore a path descending to the left and continue contouring around the slopes. 5min later, follow waymarks when the path becomes faint. Cross some sections of boulders (yellow waymarks).

2 2:35: Climb steeply for 5-10min. Then follow waymarks and cairns on an undulating path amongst more rocks. Later, keep SH at junctions, following cairns: ignore paths descending to the left.

3 3:15: Arrive at the top of the **Index ski-lift (2385m)**. Descend to les Praz using the Index and Flégère lifts.

Spectacular reflections of MB in Lac Blanc

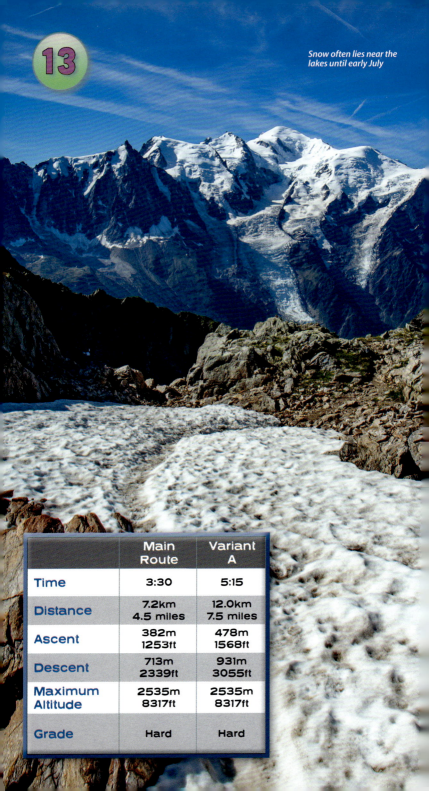

13

Snow often lies near the lakes until early July

	Main Route	Variant A
Time	3:30	5:15
Distance	7.2km 4.5 miles	12.0km 7.5 miles
Ascent	382m 1253ft	478m 1568ft
Descent	713m 2339ft	931m 3055ft
Maximum Altitude	2535m 8317ft	2535m 8317ft
Grade	Hard	Hard

Les Lacs Noirs

*The second of
les Lacs Noirs*

A tough route through rocky terrain to a pair of beautiful high altitude lakes. Les Lacs Noirs ('the black lakes') are tucked away behind a remote ridge far from the most popular walking routes of the Chamonix Valley. This means that they attract fewer visitors than the more famous Lac Blanc. Les Lacs Noirs are not quite as obviously spectacular as Lac Blanc but they are still a sight to behold and you have more chance of the solitude that many crave. If you reach the lakes early in the day, watch out for ibex.

The rocky terrain is quite challenging. Just before Col de la Glière, take care crossing a steep slope using metal railings. The route is sometimes hard to follow: watch for cairns/waymarks. Sometimes snow lies on parts of this route until early July: in such conditions navigation is difficult. Also avoid this walk in bad weather or low visibility.

> **Variant A:** Walk 13 can be combined with Walk 11, making an excellent loop. For this option, follow Walk 13 to la Parsa cable car station near Planpraz: from there, follow Walk 11 in reverse to return to the upper station of the Flégère cable car. Use the cable car to descend to Planpraz.

Start/Finish: The walk uses the Flégère and Index ski-lifts to ascend. The car park for the Flégère lift is at les Praz de Chamonix: ///lull.intention.pompom. The walk uses the Planpraz cable car to descend so you finish near Chamonix town centre.

Public Transport: Bus lines 1, 2 and V2 all stop at the start point in les Praz. There is a train station in les Praz which is a short walk from the start. At the finish, bus lines 1, 2, 3, V1 and V2 all stop at Chamonix Centre bus stop, which is a short walk from the Planpraz cable car's lower station. There are train stops near Aiguille du Midi and Chamonix town centre. If parking a car at the start in les Praz, you could use public transport to return to it at the end: alternatively, you could follow Walk 9 to head back to les Praz on foot.

Food/Drink: Les Praz de Chamonix; la Flégère; Planpraz; Chamonix

Map: 3630OT Chamonix

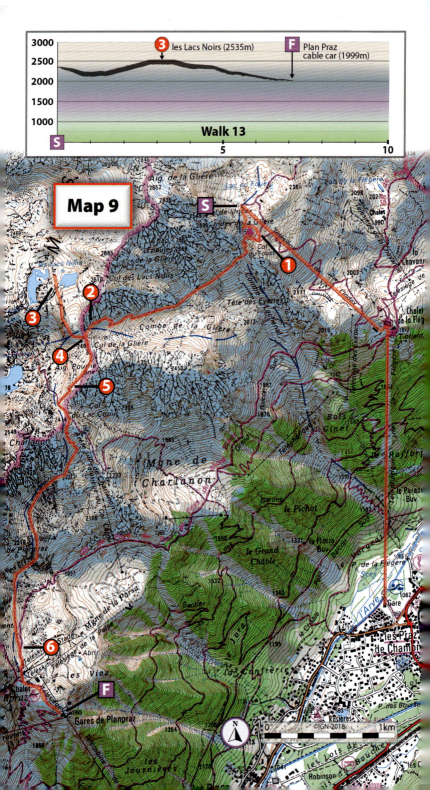

Map 9

Walk 13

3000

2500

2000 — ③ les Lacs Noirs (2535m)   F Plan Praz cable car (1999m)

1500

1000

S

5

10

The path between Col du Lac Cornu and Planpraz

S See Map 9. Ascend to **2385m** using the Flégère and Index ski-lifts. Just after exiting the lift, ignore the signpost which indicates that you should TR: you can take this route but it follows a less enjoyable ski piste. Instead, TL and pick up a path which zigzags downwards to the S.

1 0:10: TR and descend on a track. Shortly afterwards, TR at **Col du Fouet (2361m)** ('Col de la Glière') and descend on a rocky path. There are fabulous views of MB. After 10-15min, the path levels and starts to undulate. 10min later, the main climb begins: Col de la Glière can be seen up above.

2 1:00: The path cuts across a steep, rocky slope: there are metal railings to assist. Take great care. 5min later, TR at **Col de la Glière (2461m)** ('Lac Noir'): Lac Cornu (Walk 8) is visible below to the left. Now climb on a path: when it becomes faint, follow yellow waymarks and cairns.

3 1:25: Pass to the left of the first of **les Lacs Noirs (2535m)**. Follow cairns/ waymarks and a few minutes later, arrive above the second lake: often there are beautiful reflections in the water. Retrace your steps back towards Col de la Glière.

4 1:45: Keep SH at **Col de la Glière** ('Planpraz'). Shortly afterwards, descend over boulders (yellow waymarks). Afterwards, continue on a clear path. After 5-10min, cross another section of boulders (yellow waymarks).

5 2:00: Keep SH at a faint junction: there are little metal steps to help you climb a boulder. 10min later, arrive at **Col du Lac Cornu (2414m)**. Descend S on a faint, rocky path (cairns/waymarks). After 5min, take care descending a steep rocky section. Afterwards, the gradient eases and the clear path soon zigzags down the slope. TR at a junction. The views of the MB Massif are incredible.

6 3:20: TR onto a track. A few minutes later, arrive at the top of **la Parsa ski-lift (2075m)**: TL at a junction and descend on a track. 5min later, arrive at the top of the **Planpraz cable car (1999m)** which you can use to descend to Chamonix.

Aiguille Verte and les Drus seen from the 'Grand Balcon Sud'

	Main Route
Time	7:45
Distance	18.0km 11.2 miles
Ascent	1415m 4643ft
Descent	1415m 4643ft
Maximum Altitude	2352m 7717ft
Grade	Very Hard

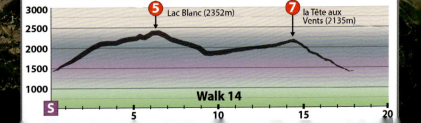

Lac Blanc (2352m)

la Tête aux Vents (2135m)

Walk 14

Lac Blanc: the Connoisseur's Route

14

An ibex on the 'Grand Balcon Sud'

This is probably the finest route to one of the most photographed places in the Alps, the superlative Lac Blanc with its incredible reflections of the MB Massif. There is a fabulous refuge beside the lake which is a great place to eat or spend the night.

However, there is much more to this epic walk than Lac Blanc: the scenery throughout is exceptional, even by the standards of the Chamonix Valley. For many hours, you will climb a spectacular ridge on a path known as the 'Grand Balcon Sud'. The views of the MB Massif are some of the best in the whole valley: the Aiguille Verte is particularly beautiful when viewed from here. You will also pass the stunning Lacs de Chéserys.

On the descent, the incredible scenes continue and you get the opportunity to use the famous and exhilarating ladders at Aiguillette d'Argentière: a long section of metal ladders, steps and railings bolted into the rock face, enabling you to climb vertically down the cliffs. The sections of ladders are the stuff of legend to hikers but, if you have a head for heights, then they are quite straightforward. However, take great care as the drops are sheer and a fall would be serious. For many this will be a highlight of the Chamonix Valley but for others it could be daunting: they are not suitable for those who have a fear of heights. Do not attempt the ladders in wet conditions.

Start/Finish: The car park half-way between Tré-le-Champ and Col des Montets: ///marina.overage.sacking. Travelling from Argentière towards Col des Montets, the car park is on the right.

Public Transport: Bus lines 2 and V2 connect Argentière with Chamonix, les Praz and le Tour. From Argentière, catch bus line 21 towards Col des Montets. Ask the driver to drop you at the car park: it is the second car park after leaving Argentière. The nearest train station is Argentière: to reach the start, you can catch bus line 21 from outside the station.

Food/Drink: Refuge du Lac Blanc; Refuge la Flégère

Map: 3630OT Chamonix

14

This walk can be undertaken in either direction and there are advantages to both options. We prefer to walk anti-clockwise, as described here, because this enables you to face MB on the long climb up the Grand Balcon Sud. On the other hand, a clockwise approach has the advantage of enabling you to tackle the ladders at Aiguillette d'Argentière by climbing rather than descending (which is probably harder).

It is fair to say that this walk is one of the most challenging in this book but it is also one of the most rewarding. In good conditions, navigation is straightforward but this is a high altitude route so avoid it in bad weather or low visibility. Often, snow lies on parts of this route until early July: in such conditions, navigation is difficult. There are some rocky sections with no path: follow waymarks and cairns.

S See Map 8 (red route line). From the car park, cross the road and pick up a path ('Lac Blanc'). A few minutes later, TL at a junction ('Lac Blanc').

1 0:15: TL at another junction ('Lac Blanc').

2 1:30: Follow cairns when the path crosses some rock slabs. 20min later, keep SH at a pyramid-shaped cairn ('Lac Blanc'). The path now levels out and you get your first glimpse of MB. Shortly afterwards, cross a section of boulders: watch your footing.

3 2:30: TR at a junction beside a large rock ('Lac Blanc') and climb: in early summer, the slopes are carpeted with the beautiful pink Alpenrose. Soon notice the first of the Lacs des Chéserys on the right. TR at another junction beside a large cairn ('Lac Blanc').

4 3:05: Follow the path around the left side of the most westerly of the **Lacs des Chéserys (2211m)**: you could also take the path heading around the right side to view the stunning reflections of the mountains in the lake. To the W of the lake, the two paths meet: now climb on a steep path. A few minutes later, climb some metal ladders: take great care although they are not as difficult as the ones you will descend later.

5 3:30: Arrive at **Lac Blanc (2352m)**. Head S on a path. After 10min, keep SH at a junction. At the next junction, TR: the descent is steep at times.

6 4:50: Arrive at a plateau, near the restaurant at **la Chavanne**: TL and head NE on a path. Alternatively, you could follow one of the tracks uphill to the S to head to the refuge at **la Flégère (1877m)**: the refuge is just below the cable car station. Climb gently to **Chalet des Chéserys (1998m)**: ignore paths on the left and right and continue NE, climbing more steeply now.

7 6:10: Arrive at the cairn at **la Tête aux Vents (2135m)**: TR and descend (initially E) on a path. Soon reach the first section of the famous ladders. Take great care as you go down the ladders, metal steps and railings. Afterwards, continue descending on a steep path. 5-10min later, descend the second section of ladders which is longer than the first. Then descend on a path. TL at a junction.

8 7:40: At **Tré-le-Champ (1417m)**, TL up the main road. Shortly afterwards, at a parking area on the left, cross the road and pick up a path running N alongside the road.

F 7:45: Arrive back at the start.

14

*The famous ladders at
Aiguillette d'Argentière*

	Main Route
Time	4:30
Distance	10.1km 6.3 miles
Ascent	860m 2822ft
Descent	860m 2822ft
Maximum Altitude	2201m 7221ft
Grade	Hard

Aiguillette des Posettes is high above the Chamonix Valley

S See Map 10 (red route line). From the parking area, head E and cross the road to some stone buildings. Pick up a path which enters forest and runs alongside the road. Soon TR ('Aiguillette des Posettes') and climb. For now, TL at any junctions following signs for 'Aiguillette des Posettes'.

1 0:50: After emerging from the trees, TR at a junction, ignoring the path to the left heading to 'Aiguillette des Posettes'. Now, at any junctions, keep heading NE ('Col des Posettes'): ignore paths to the left (which climb more directly to Aiguillette des Posettes) and to the right (which descend SE to le Tour). Eventually, pass to the left of **Chalets de Balme**.

2 2:20: TL at **Col des Posettes (1997m)**, heading SW on a path. Soon start to climb towards a ridge. When the path passes over a series of rocks, it is tricky to follow. Eventually, the path turns left and heads straight up along the top of the ridge: this section is rocky and difficult. Towards the top, the path splits a number of times but they should all head to the summit.

3 2:50: Arrive at the summit of **Aiguillette des Posettes (2201m)**. Follow the path SW down the crest of the ridge. After a few minutes, keep SH at a junction, staying on the ridge ('Col des Montets'). Soon the descent gets very steep.

4 3:50: The path bends to the left and continues descending. Keep right at any junctions.

5 4:25: Arrive back near the road: TL on a path. Shortly afterwards, the path returns to the parking area.

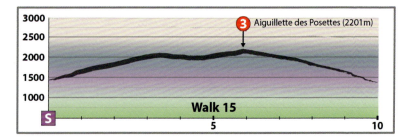

3 Aiguillette des Posettes (2201m)

Walk 15

Aiguillette des Posettes

15

The slopes are covered with Alpenrose in early summer

If you want to admire the beautiful Aiguilles Rouges, then there are few better vantage points from which to do so than Aiguillette des Posettes. It is a wild and beautiful place which is at its best in early summer when the vibrant pink Alpenrose coats the slopes. Furthermore, it is a popular haunt of chamois. The views of Glacier du Tour on the climb are magnificent.

The section from Col des Posettes to Aiguillette des Posettes is tricky to navigate as there are few waymarks and the path is not well defined. This section of the route is also exposed and should be avoided in low visibility, bad weather or snow. The descent is a real 'knee-jerker'!

Start/Finish: The parking area just NW of Tré-le-Champ: ///immense.slowly.mongrels. Travelling from Argentière towards Col des Montets, it is the first parking area on the left.

Public Transport: Bus lines 2 and V2 connect Argentière with Chamonix, les Praz and le Tour. From Argentière, catch bus line 21 towards Col des Montets: ask the driver to drop you at the car park. The nearest train station is Argentière: to reach the start, you can catch bus line 21 from outside the station.

Food/Drink: None

Map: 3630OT Chamonix

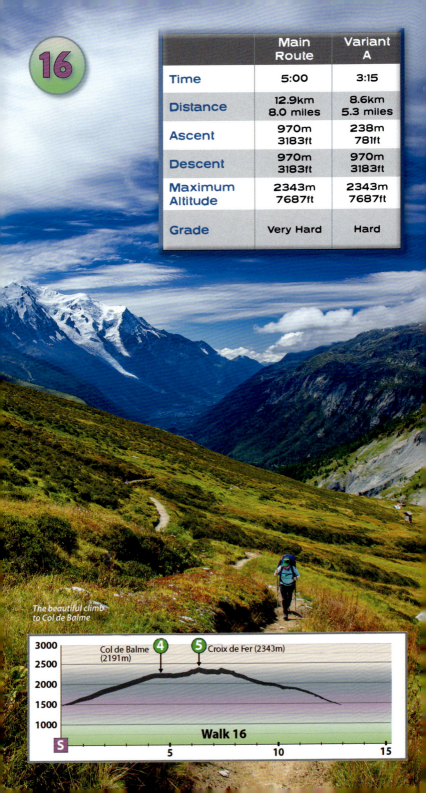

	Main Route	Variant A
Time	5:00	3:15
Distance	12.9km 8.0 miles	8.6km 5.3 miles
Ascent	970m 3183ft	238m 781ft
Descent	970m 3183ft	970m 3183ft
Maximum Altitude	2343m 7687ft	2343m 7687ft
Grade	Very Hard	Hard

16

The beautiful climb to Col de Balme

Col de Balme (2191m) · 4

Croix de Fer (2343m) · 5

Walk 16

Croix de Fer

Aiguillette des Posettes seen from near Col de Balme

A wonderful route high above the N end of the Chamonix Valley. Quickly after leaving le Tour, the views open up with the whole of the valley and the MB Massif behind you: it is breathtaking. After a long climb, reach Col de Balme, the exquisite setting for a refuge which was apparently built in 1877 and was occupied by German troops during World War 2. In front of the refuge there is a much-photographed stone marker indicating the Switzerland/France frontier. Shortly afterwards the main excitement of the day begins with a climb up a knife-edge ridge to Croix de Fer: the views into Switzerland to the N, and back down the Chamonix Valley to the S, are exquisite.

T he ridge to Croix de Fer is narrow and exposed. It should be avoided by those who have a fear of heights. There are rocky sections on the ridge and some scrambling is required. Avoid this route in low visibility, bad weather or snow.

> **Variant A:** Avoid most of the climb by using the Charamillon and Autannes ski-lifts. From the upper station of the Autannes lift (2185m), head N on a path ('Col de Balme'). 5-10min later, arrive at Waypoint No.4.

Start/Finish: The car park for the Charamillon and Autannes ski-lifts in le Tour: ///healer.spearing.gardening

Public Transport: Bus lines 2 and V2 connect le Tour with Chamonix, les Praz and Argentière. The nearest train station is Argentière: to reach le Tour, catch bus lines 2 or V2 from outside the station.

Food/Drink: Charamillon; Refuge du Col de Balme

Map: 3630OT Chamonix

S See Map 10 (green route line). From the car park, pass to the right of the lift station and climb on a track ('Col de Balme').

1 0:20: TR onto a path ('Sentier Piétons').

2 1:00: Keep SH at a track. Soon afterwards, TL at the lift station at **Charamillon**. Just afterwards, TL at a fork ('Col de Balme'). A few minutes later, TL at a fork. Soon afterwards, TR on a path, climbing quite steeply. At the next junction, TL ('Col de Balme').

3 1:55: Keep SH at a crossroads.

4 2:00: Arrive at **Refuge du Col de Balme (2191m)**. Head N on a wide path, entering Switzerland. 10-15min later, bear right at a saddle along a ridge. The path is narrow and exposed in places: take care.

5 3:00: Arrive at **Croix de Fer (2343m)**. Retrace your steps to the saddle. Then keep SH (W) on a narrow path and climb. Soon, arrive on the summit of **Tête de Balme (2321m)**. Descend to the SW on a narrow path. At a ski-lift, pick up a wide path and zigzag down to the SW: pass back and forth under the cables a few times.

6 3:50: Keep SH (S) when you meet a track: do not TL. Shortly afterwards, near **Col des Posettes (1997m)**, TL at a junction of tracks heading S. 5min later, TL at a junction.

7 4:30: At the **Charamillon** lift station, TR and descend on a track. Shortly afterwards, keep SH on a path. 15-20min later, TL and descend on a track.

F 5:00: 5min later, arrive back at the start.

The refuge at Col de Balme
has an exquisite setting

	Main Route
Time	4:15
Distance	9.2km 5.7 miles
Ascent	566m 1857ft
Descent	896m 2940ft
Maximum Altitude	2702m 8865ft
Grade	Medium

17

Refuge Albert 1st is situated beside Glacier du Tour

Charamillon (1912m) **F**

4 Refuge Albert 1st (2702m)

Walk 17

S

3000
2500
2000
1500
1000

5   10

Refuge Albert 1st

The path passes right next to Glacier du Tour

As far as glacier walks go, this is one of the finest. An incredible balcony path leads you around slopes covered with Alpenrose and Myrtille: there are spectacular views of Glacier du Tour and MB throughout. In fact, you get so close to the glacier that you can see every serac and crevice. With all this splendour on show, the refuge itself is almost an afterthought but the panorama from its terrace is wonderful. The walk could be combined with an unforgettable overnight stay at the refuge.

Navigation is straightforward except that there are a few places where the path disappears over rocks and boulders: follow waymarks carefully. Avoid this route in low visibility, bad weather or snow. The final approach to the refuge is steep and rocky.

Start/Finish: The walk takes advantage of the Charamillon and Autannes ski-lifts to ascend. The car park for the ski-lift is in le Tour: ///healer.spearing.gardening. Use the Charamillon ski-lift to descend.

Public Transport: Bus lines 2 and V2 connect le Tour with Chamonix, les Praz and Argentière. The nearest train station is Argentière: to reach le Tour, catch bus lines 2 or V2 from outside the station.

Food/Drink: Charamillon; Refuge Albert 1st

Map: 3630OT Chamonix

S See Map 10 (orange route line). Ascend to **2185m** using the Charamillon and Autannes ski-lifts. Head S on a path which contours around the hillside, climbing gently ('Refuge Albert 1'). The views of MB and the Aiguilles Rouges are already very fine.

1 0:30: Keep SH at a junction: the path on the right will be the path of your descent. 10min later, as you round a corner, Glacier du Tour comes into view.

2 1:00: Descend a few steep sections of rocks: there are railings to assist. 10-15min later, the path enters a zone of glacial moraine: there are sections of boulders to cross. Soon, the path bends left and climbs a rocky spur right beside the glacier.

3 2:10: Climb over boulders again: follow red waymarks carefully. Just below the refuge, climb some rocks.

4 2:20: Arrive at **Refuge Albert 1st (2702m)**. Now retrace your steps.

1 3:45: At Waypoint No.1, TL and descend ('le Tour').

F 4:15: Arrive at the **Charamillon ski station**. Use the lift to descend to the start

The balcony path offers amazing views of the Aiguilles Rouges

18

The views of the Aiguilles Rouges on the descent

	Main Route	Variant A
Time	6:00	3:30
Distance	13.7km 8.5 miles	8.2km 5.1 miles
Ascent	1110m 3642ft	389m 1276ft
Descent	1110m 3642ft	1110m 3642ft
Maximum Altitude	2338m 7671ft	2338m 7671ft
Grade	Hard	Medium

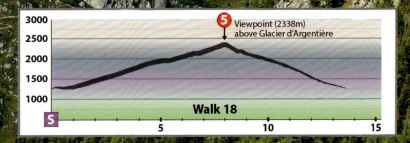

5 Viewpoint (2338m) above Glacier d'Argentière

Walk 18

S

Glacier d'Argentière

18

The amazing viewpoint above Glacier d'Argentière

This is another Chamonix Valley classic. The climb through the forest is long but it will be quickly forgotten when you reach the magnificent viewpoint beside Glacier d'Argentière. The descent is even more scenic because, as well as enjoying more fabulous glacier views, you face the beautiful Aiguilles Rouges all the way down.

After la Croix de Lognan, there are some steep, rocky sections but they are not too difficult. The descent along the rocky spur (after Waypoint No.5) is steep and unstable in places: watch your footing. Waymarking is poor between la Croix de Lognan and Refuge de Lognan.

> **Variant A:** To shorten the route, use the Grands Montets cable car to ascend to la Croix de Lognan (Waypoint No.3): this cuts out about two thirds of the climb. At the time of writing, the cable car was closed following a fire.

Start/Finish: The car park for the Grands Montets cable car, near Argentière: ///await.guitars.kindled

Public Transport: Bus line 2 connects the Grand Montets car park with Chamonix, les Praz, Argentière and le Tour. The nearest train station is Argentière: to reach the start, you can catch bus line 2 from outside the station.

Food/Drink: Restaurant at la Croix de Lognan; Refuge de Lognan

Map: 3630OT Chamonix

The village of Argentière

Map 11
©IGN-2018
0 1km

S See Map 11. Head E on a tarmac lane just to the left of the Grands Montets cable car station ('Petit Balcon Nord'). Soon, pass to the right of another cable car station. A few minutes later, TR and go through a circular tunnel, now heading S. 5min later, TL onto a track. Just afterwards, TR on a path ('la Croix de Lognan') which soon passes some chalets and starts to climb.

1 0:20: Just where the path starts to descend, ignore a path on the left. 50m further on, TL ('la Croix de Lognan') and head through forest on a small path: stay on the main path, following yellow signs.

2 2:00: After a chalet, TR and climb on a track. Shortly after the track bends left, TL at a junction of tracks.

3 2:20: Pass some ski-lifts and just afterwards, reach the cable car station at **la Croix de Lognan (1973m)**. Head SE on a ski piste: it soon bends left to head E. 15-20min later, keep SH at a junction. A few minutes later, TR at a fork and climb steeply on a rocky piste.

4 3:00: When you meet a track, TR and climb. Shortly afterwards, TR onto another track.

5 3:30: Arrive at the spectacular **viewpoint (2338m)** above Glacier d'Argentière. After taking a break to soak in the vista, head back down the path briefly. After 50m, bear right on a path which quickly climbs onto a little spur and then descends along the spine of it. After descending a steep rocky section, arrive at another fabulous viewpoint. Head W and pick up a broad path. Shortly afterwards, TR on a path down a spur to another excellent viewpoint. From there, descend W on a winding track. There are amazing views of the Aiguilles Rouges across the valley.

6 4:20: Keep SH at a junction. Shortly afterwards, TR on a path. A few minutes later, arrive at **Refuge de Lognan (2032m)**: from the terrace, descend W on a path.

7 5:00: TR onto a track, still descending: the surface is loose so watch your step.

F 6:00: Arrive back at the start.

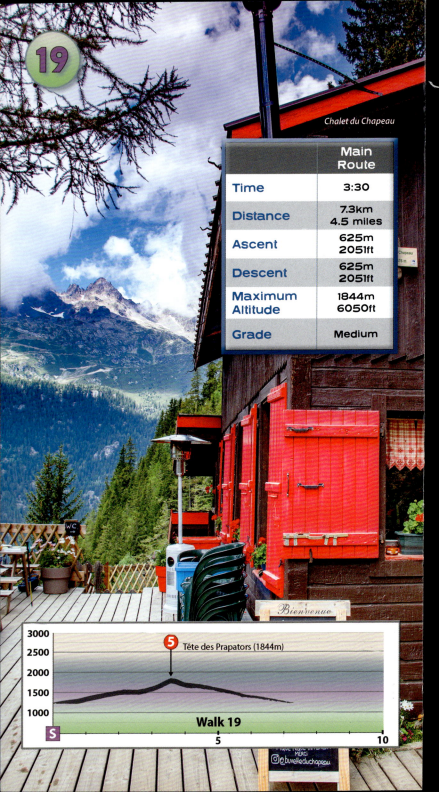

19

Chalet du Chapeau

	Main Route
Time	3:30
Distance	7.3km 4.5 miles
Ascent	625m 2051ft
Descent	625m 2051ft
Maximum Altitude	1844m 6050ft
Grade	Medium

5 Tête des Prapators (1844m)

Walk 19

S

5   10

Le Chapeau

The lovely waterfall at Waypoint No.2

A beautiful route offering some excellent views of the Mer de Glace and its surrounding peaks. The views of Chamonix and the W side of the valley are also excellent.

T he route mostly uses clear paths. However, between Waypoints No.3 and 5, take care as the path is often steep and/or narrow and the drops are sheer: there are some ladders and railings to assist. There are also a few short sections of rocks to climb over: these are not too difficult but should be avoided in wet weather. Navigation is straightforward.

Start/Finish: The car park just S of the hamlet of le Lavancher: ///routs.provisional.vessels

Public Transport: Bus lines 2 and V2 connect le Lavancher with Chamonix, les Praz, Argentière and le Tour. The bus stop is beside the main road: to reach the start, leave the main road and climb on 'Route du Lavancher'. This road winds up through the hamlet until it eventually arrives at the car park. The nearest train station is les Tines: to reach the start of the walk from the station, head briefly up the main road. Then TR on a track. After 5min, TL and climb on a path. 15-20min later, reach the road just above the car park at le Lavancher.

Food/Drink: Chalet du Chapeau

Map: 3630OT Chamonix

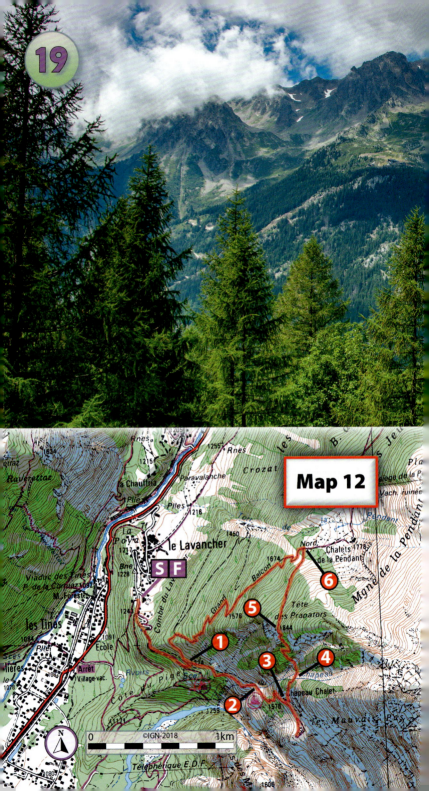

Map 12

©IGN-2018

0   1km

The wonderful views of the W side of the Chamonix Valley

S See Map 12. From the car park, climb S up the road. A few minutes later, TR onto a path, climbing through trees ('le Chapeau'). A few minutes later, TR onto another path ('le Chapeau'). Soon, TL at a fork, still climbing.

1 0:20: A few minutes later, TR at another junction ('le Chapeau'). 5min later, TR at a fork (yellow waymark).

2 0:50: Pass a magnificent waterfall: move as quickly as safety allows as this area is prone to rockfalls.

3 1:00: Arrive at **Chalet du Chapeau (1576m)**: keep climbing on the path. 5min later, keep SH at a junction ('Point de Vue sur le Glacier'). 10min later, arrive at the viewpoint. Unfortunately, the glacier has now receded so much that there is little of it to see: the mountain views are spectacular though. Retrace your steps back to the previous junction: TR ('Tête des Prapators'). As you climb, the views of the glacier get better: the ice-field is visible. Take care as the path is very narrow in places and the drops are steep.

4 1:35: Soon after crossing a stream, the gradient increases and there are some railings and ladders to assist. Then climb a short section of rocks.

5 2:05: Keep SH across **Tête des Prapators (1844m)** and descend through trees.

6 2:25: TL at a junction ('le Lavancher'): this path is known as the 'Grand Balcon Nord'. Keep SH on the main path, ignoring offshoots. When you reach Waypoint No.1 again, keep SH (downhill). Keep SH at subsequent junctions as you retrace your steps.

F 3:30: Arrive back at the car park.

View of les Drus from Montenvers

	Main Route	Variant A
Time	4:45	2:45
Distance	11.1km 6.9 miles	5.5km 3.4 miles
Ascent	815m 2674ft	815m 2674ft
Descent	815m 2674ft	0m 0ft
Maximum Altitude	1913m 6277ft	1913m 6277ft
Grade	Hard	Medium

Variant A: to avoid the descent, you could return to Chamonix from Montenvers using the Montenvers Tramway.

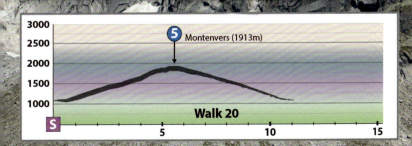

Montenvers (1913m)

Walk 20

Mer de Glace (via Buvette des Mottets)

Buvette le Caillet

Everyone who visits the Chamonix Valley wants to see the famous Mer de Glace which is the main attraction on this fabulous walk. Although the glacier has receded substantially in recent years, it is undeniably impressive and is overlooked by a range of magnificent peaks. The high point is Montenvers where there is a variety of attractions including the Ice Cave, a crystal gallery, a souvenir shop and places to eat: the huge open terrace of the restaurant is spectacular.

Although it is busy at Montenvers, the rest of the walk is less hectic: most people arrive at Montenvers by tram from Chamonix. Buvette des Mottets is a wonderful place with a magnificent setting overlooking the distinct summit of les Drus. It is well worth stopping there for a drink.

Large parts of the climb and descent are in shady, aromatic forest so it is a good route for a hot day. There are a number of paths to chose from in this area so follow signposts carefully. The paths are often steep and rocky. There is a short section without a clear path just before the buvette: follow cairns and faint waymarks. The path between Buvette des Mottets and Montenvers is rocky, uneven and hard to follow in places: take care. There is also a short ladder bolted into the rocks. From mid-September onwards, hunting is permitted in the forests in this area on certain days of the week: it is advisable to wear some bright clothing.

Start/Finish: 'Chemin de la Source de l'Arveyron', les Praz de Chamonix: ///scam.brags.ourselves

Public Transport: Bus lines 1, 2 and V2 all stop in les Praz: from the village centre, walk to les Praz train station. From the train station, it is a 15min walk to the start: head E and then NE on 'Route des Gaudenays' which eventually becomes 'Chemin de la Source de l'Arveyron'.

Food/Drink: Les Praz de Chamonix; Buvette des Mottets; Montenvers; Buvette le Caillet

Map: 3630OT Chamonix

S See Map 1 (blue route line). From an information board, head SE on 'Chemin des Rantourneurs'. Follow signs for 'Sentier du Granite'. After 5min, cross the River l'Arveyron on a bridge and then TR on a path. Shortly afterwards, TR at a junction.

1 0:10: Shortly afterwards, TL and climb on a broad path (no signpost).

2 1:10: TL at a junction ('Montenvers par les Mottets').

3 1:40: Climb some wooden steps. Shortly afterwards, the path bears right, becoming faint (red waymarks). 5min later, arrive at the magnificent buvette at **Rochers des Mottets (1638m)** which serves drinks and meals. You can also stay the night in fixed tents perched precariously on the edge of the slopes or suspended from the trees. TR at the buvette ('Montenvers') and follow cairns, waymarks and signs over rock slabs. Afterwards, climb a short metal ladder and continue upwards on a clear path.

4 2:10: TL at a junction ('Montenvers'): ignore the path to the right which also heads to Montenvers. Now the route is hard to follow as it winds its way between boulders: it is quite hard work.

5 2:40: TR at a fork, climbing. 5-10min later, arrive at the restaurant and viewing platform at **Montenvers**. After enjoying the views, keep SH passing the tram station. Then head through a tunnel under the tracks. TL before the hotel and head around the left side of it. At the Chamonix Valley side of the hotel, pick up a path descending alongside the tram tracks. Soon, keep SH, ignoring a faint path on the right (which is signposted to 'Rochers des Mottets'). A few minutes later, TL at a junction ('Chamonix par Caillet').

7 3:10: Cross the train tracks and descend on a path.

8 3:30: TR ('les Praz') at **Buvette le Caillet (1590m)**.

2 3:50: Arrive back at the junction at Waypoint No.2: keep SH (crossing a track) and descend on the path travelled earlier. Now retrace your steps.

F 4:45: Arrive back at the start.

The panorama from the terrace of the restaurant at Montenvers

Glacier de Taconnaz (Walk 2)

Notes

Notes